A CONNOISSEUR'S GUIDE TO ANTIQUE

POTTERY & PORCELAIN

A CONNOISSEUR'S GUIDE TO ANTIQUE
POTTERY &
PORCELAIN

RONALD PEARSALL

SMITHMARK

This edition published in 1997 by SMITHMARK Publishers,
a division of U.S. Media Holdings, Inc., 115 West 18th Street,
New York, NY 10011.

SMITHMARK books are available for bulk purchase for sales
promotion and premium use. For details write or call the manager
of special sales, SMITHMARK Publishers, 115 West 18th Street,
New York, NY 10011.

This book was designed and produced by
Todtri Productions Limited P.O. Box 572, New York,
NY 10116-0572 FAX: (212) 695-6688

Printed and bound in Singapore

Library of Congress Catalog Card Number 97-066055
ISBN 0-7651-9235-7

Author: Ronald Pearsall

Publisher: Robert M. Tod
Designer: Vic Giolitto
Art Director: Ron Pickless
Editor: Nicolas Wright
Typeset and DTP: Blanc Verso/UK

CONTENTS

INTRODUCTION

Opposite: Founded in 1710, Meissen was the first (and for the first fifty years, the best) porcelain factory in Europe. It set the highest of standards and its products were even emulated in China, whose own porcelain Meissen set out to copy. The glory of Meissen were the painters and the modellers, the latter assuming the greater importance in 1733, with the arrival of J. J. Kändler. As chief modeller, he obtained artistic control of the factory's output. Meissen could be grand or intimate, as in this pair of waxwings, a passerine (sparrow-like) bird native to Bavaria, of about 1741.

I n certain realms of antiques there is only so much to know. Someone with a little diligence can find out everything there is to know about corkscrews. But pottery and porcelain know no limits; there is no conceivable subject with as much variety, from the classic beauty of Greek vases and the odd throw-away pottery of medieval times, to the classic period of porcelain, the excesses of the nineteenth century, the brief explosion of art pottery and Art Nouveau, and on to the sheer joy and exuberance of Art Deco in the 1920s and 1930s.

There are the eccentrics, there are the master potters, and there are the thousands of pottery painters, known and mostly unknown, who brought their skills to that most appreciative of materials—clay. For that is what pottery and porcelain is all about—clay with added extras. Sometimes just one addition (such as potash), sometimes dozens. Something can be made from clay in a few minutes, or it can take months, building up a vase piece by piece, which might then collapse into fragments when fired in a kiln. Clay offers a voyage of discovery for everyone. Potters learn new skills, find out new processes by sheer accident, discover new colours (perhaps by adding iron, for instance). Painters ascertain what they can and cannot do. Pottery factories develop ever more sophisticated techniques. And there is also a voyage of discovery for collectors, from the youngest to the oldest, the poorest to the richest.

Even the humble cup and saucer can be an artistic accomplishment. Not many works of art can be used day in, day out, year after year. And even in these days of multimedia and the highest of high-tech, there are few people without a favourite vase or a little figurine that brings back memories, no matter that the item claiming a place in the heart is a mass-produced piece of nonsense, the monetary value of which is of no importance at all. We may be amazed at some grand concoction of museum quality; we may even have one.

Right: Lustre ware is the decoration on pottery and porcelain by means of thin films of metal, such as copper and gold (which produces pink lustre). Josiah Wedgwood experimented with this process from 1790, and this eventually resulted in his magical "fairyland" and "moonlight" lustres. Mixing the lustre with oil produced splash lustre, much used in Sunderland ware with pictures of ships and bridges. The greatest exponent of lustre was perhaps the maker of this marvellous piece, William de Morgan (1839–1917), a master of carefully integrated flat patterns, which were stylised and richly opulent, often incorporating Greek or Cretan motifs. He retired in 1905 to become a best-selling novelist.

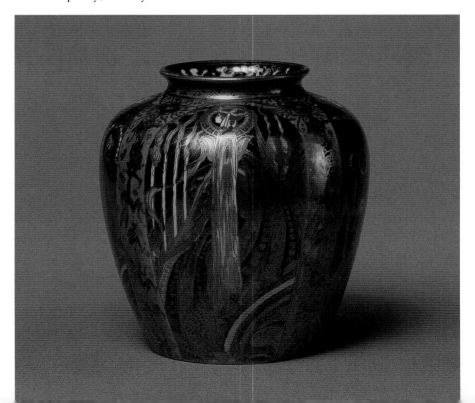

CHAPTER ONE

POTTERY'S FORMATIVE YEARS

Only the thinnest of lines separates pottery from porcelain, and sometimes it is so blurred that the old perception that porcelain is somehow "better" than pottery becomes impossible to sustain. There is no early porcelain. Adept as the ancient world was at creating fine furniture, jewellery, and delicate items of gold and silver, it could not make porcelain.

Pottery, however, was easy to produce. In hot countries clay could merely be laid out in the sun to bake. A lump of clay could be shaped with the fingers, or sausages of clay could be built up into the form of a pot or other container. More advanced civilisations used a potter's wheel (beginning about 3000 B.C.), on which the clay spun around and was shaped by the hand and by centrifugal force. Or clay could be moulded by hand. The piece was then fired at a constant heat in a kiln, introduced about 6000 B.C.

The object was still not waterproof so it needed to be glazed, after which it was fired again. Ancient civilisations used alkaline (soda glass) and lead glazes, along with other substances such as tin and later salt. Glazes could be in liquid or powdered form, and decoration could be applied in any form at any stage. The possibilities of pottery soon appeared endless. Ethnic pottery is immensely diverse, often executed with great skill, and pieces for magical and ceremonial use have a brooding power almost unequalled in later times. Throughout the world, from the cradle of civilisation in Mesopotamia to the Aztecs and Incas more than two thousand years later, the techniques were much the same, and there is even a crossover in designs and motifs.

Greek Vases

Some cultures advanced further. The beauty of Greek vases, both in shape and ornamentation, has not been surpassed. It was more than two thousand years before pottery of this quality was made again in Europe. No account exists of the precise processes used by the ancient Greeks. Their pottery is predominantly black or red, simply because the oxides of iron that exist in Greek clays produce these colours. It was soon found that if the particles of clay are fine enough they will produce a sheen, but fineness cannot be acquired through washing, so chemicals such as potash were added. The highest firing temperature possible was about 950 degrees Centigrade, and the firing was done in three stages. By careful management, the

Opposite: A pair of Vienna Etruscan vases featuring ladies playing music and dancing. The Etruscan style was invented about 1774 by Robert Adam, and was based on ancient Greek models, which were at that time supposed to be Etruscan. Etruria was an area in northwest Italy that included Tuscany; their people, the Etruscans, came from Asia Minor. A distinct Etruscan culture emerged in the eighth century B.C., reached its peak in the sixth, and then declined. The Etruscans spoke a non-Indo-European language that has not been interpreted, which has added to their mystique.

Above: A handsome container from Syria dating from about 3000 B.C., with perfect proportions and free-hand geometric decoration. It has an unpretentiousness which was somehow lost in the succeeding centuries as technology improved.

resultant object could be both black and red. These tricky processes were completely mastered in the sixth to the fourth centuries B.C.

The glory of Greek pottery lies not only in the exquisite shapes but the decoration. The greatest artists participated, perfecting superb line drawings, often of the human figure and of mythological scenes. A favourite decorative motif was the key pattern, used for friezes and edging. Foreign influences, especially from Syria, brought in a new range of subjects, including lotus flowers, bulls, lions, and goats. Two-dimensional designs gradually became three-dimensional, and extra colours were found and used.

By the fifth century B.C. Greek expertise was being introduced into Italy, but the Romans were not interested in advancing the art. Their talents were employed elsewhere, such as in conquering the known world.

Chinese Pottery and Porcelain

Thousands of miles away the Chinese were following a route of their own. Records date back to the Shang dynasty (1766–1122 B.C.). The Chinese used the potter's wheel, advanced kilns, and glazing. By using glazes containing metal oxides they could produce a range of colours.

Best known of early Chinese ware are the famous terra-cotta armies of the Han dynasty (206 B.C.–A.D. 220). In the Tang dynasty (A.D. 618–907), mass-production methods were used for press-moulding different parts. The Tang dynasty produced the marvellous multicoloured horses made to accompany the dead into the hereafter instead of real horses, but the period is best remembered for the invention of porcelain.

Above: A Greek cylix (a shallow bowl with a stem later renamed a tazza) with Apollo playing a lyre and being listened to by a bird, probably a raven. Apollo was not only the god of music, but of Greek civilization, Most, if not all, nations have myths, but no other nation than Greece has imparted to them such immortal charm and stimulated such universal interest. Dating from about 480 B.C., this cylix is especially interesting, as it indicates that the Greeks had found out how to make white pottery of quality.

Opposite: A double-handled Greek vase of about 500 B.C., found at Vulci, featuring a stylised horse with rider and attendants. The horse, as in China, provided illustrators and modellers with the opportunity to be truly creative, and whereas human figures are inclined to be stereotyped, the horses are dealt with individualistically. Around the neck of the vase is fine semi-abstract decoration.

Previous pages, left: Recent excavations have succeeded in presenting the world with a host of pottery masterpieces. These are from the tomb of Ch'in Shih-Huang-Ti and date from about 210 B.C.

Previous pages, right: A Figure, possibly a pregnant woman, on a horse, perhaps Lao-Tzu-T'ang dynasty A.D. 618–907. The most significant feature of this Chinese figure is the modelling of the horse—especially the legs, a masterpiece of observation.

Opposite: The detail of a Ch'in Shih-Huang-Ti warrior, 210 B.C., showing the vigour with which the work was carried out. Of particular interest is the absolute realism of the face, and the way the eyes are treated. A lifelike impression can be achieved by having a hole where the pupil should be. Also note the strong hands; all the fingers are the same length to supplement the feeling of strength and power.

Below: A Neolithic Chinese urn of about 2500 B.C. with geometric decoration.

It is difficult to think of any process in which the Chinese were not first on the scene. Adding ashes of tin to a clear lead glaze made buff-coloured pottery white, permitting a variety of colours to be painted on it directly. This process, known as maiolica, spread through Persia and the Middle East into Moorish-influenced Spain (with the Hispano-Moresque tradition), and thence throughout Europe, where it was eagerly seized upon as a substitute for the mysterious porcelain.

Persia and the Middle East were not just stopovers. Persian pottery is mind-shattering in its glory and gorgeous colour. Since Islam forbids the employment of the human figure in art, the use of pattern and calligraphy was pursued with tremendous skill and incomparable expertise. It is probable that the Chinese skills arrived in the Middle East in A.D. 751, when Chinese prisoners arrived in Samarkand. Lustre painting was practised by A.D. 772. Middle Eastern pottery is unique, as distinct from Chinese and European models as are the languages, and the most common objects exported to or found in the West—the large tiles and the plates—are incomparable. Birds, animals, and flowers vie with Koran quotations and meld with them. Except in Lowestoft porcelain and occasionally in Sunderland lustre, western writing and calligraphy adds little to the overall impact of a piece. In Persian and other Middle Eastern pottery, it is an integral part of it.

The endless variety of Chinese pottery and porcelain is overwhelming. Items from the Yuan dynasty (1206–1368) resemble art pottery that would not have looked out of place on an Edwardian mantelpiece. Ming dynasty pieces (1368–1644) in robust colour schemes can look like Art Deco–type animals. And the exquisite Chinese

Right: A jar from the Yangshao culture of about 4500 B.C., hand-shaped but still remarkably good-looking. The decoration is minimal, though the potter has put on a rim, which shows certain abilities and an awareness that a simple pot could be more than just a container.

Opposite: Glazed polychrome pottery camel of the Tang dynasty of the eighth century A.D. Once complete proficiency at producing finely modelled animal figures is attained, there is always the danger that the craftsman will begin "prettifying" them. Fortunately, that is not the case here. It appears to be a Bactrian two-humped camel from the deserts of central Asia.

monochrome pieces in the most subtle colours and shapes have parallels with twentieth-century masterworks by minimalist potters.

The Chinese also produced work of the greatest complexity and sophistication through their mastery of enamelling techniques. These techniques, developed from about the year 1200, enabled them to paint ceramics in "solid" overglaze colours with the utmost delicacy and precision, at first with a limited range of red, green, and yellow, and later with brown and black as well. Colour schemes have been given convenient labels, which are often confusing. Famille verte (the green family) was introduced during the reign of Kangxi (1661–1722), *famille rose* (the rose family), about 1720. European importers particularly liked *famille rose*.

What the Europeans wanted was not what the Chinese made for themselves. The West increasingly desired exotica with decoration oozing from every available surface, and if the Chinese were insufficiently acquainted with life in the West they were sent drawings and engravings to copy. From the 1500s, soon after Portugal began trading with China, the Chinese did produce what the Europeans wanted, including armorial ware depicting coats of arms. And of course Europe (and America from 1784) wanted blue-and-white porcelain.

Japanese Pottery and Porcelain

Surprisingly the Japanese lagged behind the Chinese in invention, receiving their technical knowledge via Korea, though they produced porcelain well ahead of the Europeans. Japanese ware is often unmarked, unlike Chinese ceramics; but sometimes these marks are misleading because later potters used the marks of previous potters as a mark of respect, even reverence.

The simple, sparsely decorated pieces for the Japanese tea ceremony differ immensely from the lavish often overdecorated Imari and Satsuma ware intended for the European market after Commodore Perry forced Japan to reopen trade with the outside world in 1854. Many products from Japan greatly appealed to Europeans: "Japanese" screens, parasols, and lacquered furniture cluttered up many a middle-class drawing room in the Western world.

The pottery and especially the porcelain the Japanese made for themselves is magnificent, especially that produced in Arita, a small town on the island of Kyushu. It displays a wit and energy largely lacking in Chinese ware, particularly in the figure and animal models, where people, tigers, and other creatures have a cartoonlike character and vigour. The beauty and refinement of the painted flowers, trees, animals, and birds is almost without parallel.

Above: A three-colour plate from northern Mesopotamia, the cradle of western civilization, dating from 5500–5000 B.C. The potter's wheel was invented in Mesopotamia, first made of wood, later of clay; its use spread, first of all to Egypt. The design of this plate shows incredible sophistication, considering the early date.

Opposite: Excavated from Syria, this terra-cotta container of about 2000 B.C. bears a lively grotesque, the kind of folk art that has existed throughout the ages. This style can be seen at its peak in medieval cathedrals and churches, as well as in ethnic art throughout the world.

Right: A stoneware pot from Korea, with refined decoration of human figures dancing, dating from the fifth or sixth century A.D. The banded rim is worth noting, as is the base with its cut-out sections.

Left: A Roman jug from the third century B.C. with a well-designed spout and a base decorated with hand-painted spiral motifs. The most notable type of Roman pottery is terra sigillata, a ware covered with a red gloss. The pottery provided a cheap alternative to metal cups, bowls, vases, etc., from which they derived in form and decoration, and spread throughout the Roman Empire, each subject nation adding its own motifs. These motifs in turn influenced Roman design in Italy. The spirals may have been Celtic in inspiration.

Opposite: A Roman terra-cotta oil lamp depicting a horse with accompanying rider. It has an abstract design on the rim. This lamp is of Tunisian extraction and was probably regionally made.

Early Ceramics in Europe

Opposite: Hispano-Moresque ware is a name given to lustre pottery produced in southern Spain, especially Malaga and Paterna from the thirteenth century and Valencia from the fifteenth century. These pieces were the first ceramics of any real merit to be made in Europe since classical times, and sparked off the development of maiolica in Italy. Decoration was partly Islamic, partly European, and sometimes included Islamic inscriptions, which the Spanish decorators turned into a meaningless pattern. Only scholars will be able to determine whether the roundel in the centre of this dish, which is Valencian of the fifteenth century, has a meaning or not.

Early European ceramics belong to another world. Since pottery in medieval Europe was chiefly meant for hard use in store rooms and kitchens, surviving items are mainly jugs, sometimes with a simple slip (clay of the consistency of cream) applied to them. They do not seem to have been valued or handed down, and much of our knowledge comes from excavations. Nonutilitarian pottery is found in encaustic tiles in churches and cathedrals, moulded with formal or heraldic designs. The small sizes of excavated kilns indicate that potteries were small, and it is likely that the potters themselves were nomadic, probably basing themselves at places where there was a good supply of suitable clay.

Occasionally a flash of innovation appears to clash with the general historical trend, such as the mysterious earthenware of Saint Porchaire made at Poitou or the Medici "porcelain" made in Florence between 1575 and 1587, too exclusive to be commercial propositions. This porcelain is one of the early instances of the use of experimental compounds—white clay, white sand, powdered rock crystal, or calcined lead and tin, coated with a thick lead glaze after painting and firing. The body is not pure white, but yellowish or greyish; only fifty-nine pieces survive. The shapes of the vessels derive from those of the well-established maiolica.

Among the most important and attractive of all early ware is the Hispano-Moresque tin-glazed pottery (maiolica), made from about the twelfth century (surviving specimens except in fragments are rare before the fifteenth) and originating

Below: Discovered in 1997 during an archaeological dig at Ham Hill, Somerset, England, this simple bowl features abstract incised decoration—the easiest to apply. Such discoveries are notoriously difficult to date, but this probably belongs to the Iron Age culture (which arrived in Europe about 800 B.C.). Dating is often determined by the existence of accompanying artefacts.

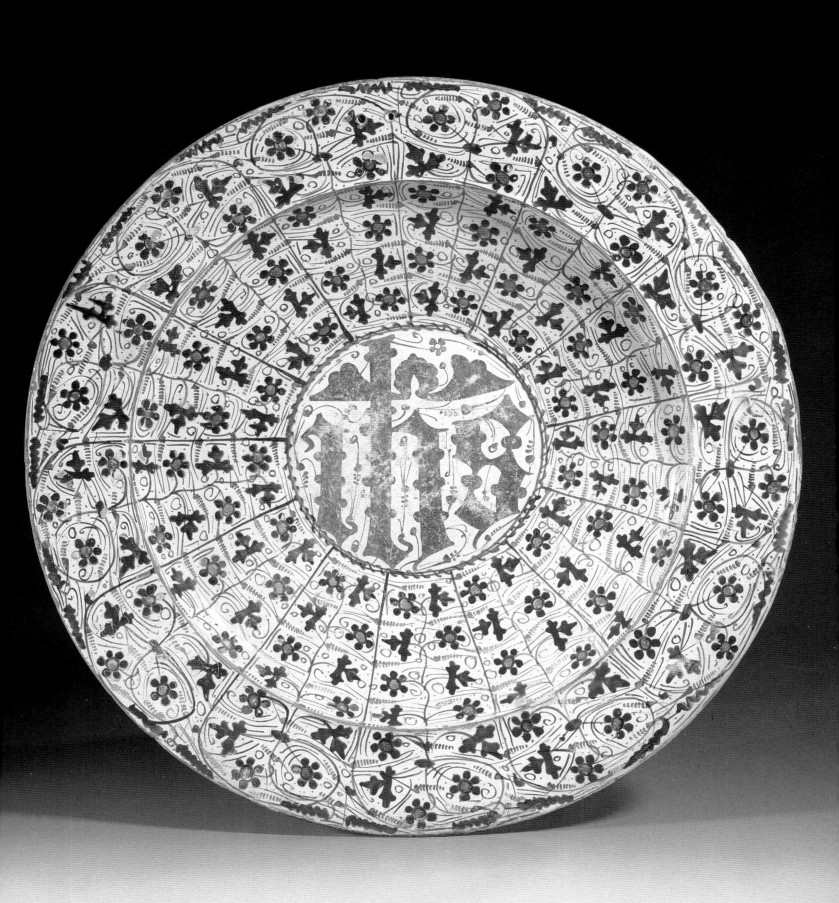

in China and filtering through the Middle East. Italy was the centre of maiolica in the fifteenth century, creating ware that was opulent and rich, with gorgeous colour. Italy also produced one of the first names in Western pottery—Luca Della Robbia (1399–1482).

The art moved into France (known there as faience) and Holland and from there to England, where it acquired the name delft (from Delft in Holland). When a French edict of 1689 (repeated in 1709) ordered the melting down of all silver and gold table vessels because the precious metals were desperately needed to make coinage, maiolica replaced silver on the tables of the wealthy. So many factories opened in France to cater to the huge demand that a fuel shortage threatened.

Both decorative and useful, delft included blue-and-white tiles and dinner services from Holland and great plaques and vases from Italy and France. Dutch painters and potters could not compete with the German and French products and Dutch delft went into decline about 1725. By 1800 maiolica had become a fringe, peasant-oriented craft. By the nineteenth century only two tin-glazed factories survived in Delft; the technique was revived in 1876 with only limited success.

Between 1745 and 1750, the emerging years of porcelain, new techniques resulted in "enamel colours" of a richness previously unknown. Imported Chinese blue-and-white china was widely imitated, though not wisely since it brought out the

Above: A pair of jardinieres of fine workmanship from the Nevers pottery, which was established in France in 1588. The potters drew inspiration from the works of great painters such as Poussin, and also from Chinese models from about 1644, as here. These jardinieres date from about 1670 and are in what is known as the Bleu Persan style. Shortly afterwards, the pottery was eclipsed by those at Rouen and Moustiers, and Nevers became imitative. Nevers is renowned for the exquisite colour schemes it used.

Opposite: A German maiolica dish bearing a coat of arms of an abbreviated sort and an odd medley of what appear to be military motifs, including cannon, cannon balls, and flags, which have been rendered in perspective. Although the Italians invented maiolica (tin-glazed pottery), its use spread throughout Europe, where it was variously named faience, fayence, and delft. The British preferred delft (from Delft in Holland). The range of colours in this German dish (which in Britain would have been called a charger) is unfortunate; maiolica was especially suited to blue and white.

flaws of maiolica. Tin-glazing results in a brittle edge on flatware and the glaze flakes off, as owners of delft plates know only too well

Dutch delft had the greatest influence on British ware, largely because of the close trading links, partly brought about by the restoration of the monarchy in England after the Civil War. Charles II, who had been exiled in Europe, encouraged European influences. English delft includes barbers' bowls with a segment cut out in the rim (barbers, who were also surgeons, used the bowls to catch the blood), drug jars of great charm, and "chargers" (large decorative plates) with bold, free painting. Spontaneity was essential since the decoration had to be applied while the tin glaze was still absorbent. There were several production centres; the most important were Lambeth, Bristol, and Liverpool. Few items of English delft are marked.

One of the outstanding early potters working with lead glazes was the Frenchman Bernard Palissy (active in the late sixteenth century), noted for his naturalistic and slightly creepy animals. Lead glazes could be stained with metal oxides and were often combined with slip (liquid clay of the consistency of cream), which could be trailed across an object or built up architecturally.

Slip was widely used in English ware from the seventeenth century. One of the earliest centres was Wrotham in Kent, where multihandled jugs, mugs, and candlesticks were made. Staffordshire potteries refined the techniques, and there were potters of great innovation such as the Toft family. These wares were peculiarly English, as was Jackfield, a red-clay body entirely covered with a glossy black glaze,

Above: To many, blue and white pottery and porcelain is quintessentially English. This unusual nursing bottle is typical of the way in which almost anything could serve as a surface for scenes, the variety of which is incredible and covers every possible category, from simple rustic subjects, as here, to topical themes.

Opposite: Maiolica was especially suitable for elaborate groupings, and this was exploited in the nineteenth century when the English pottery factories evolved majolica. The name is a corruption of the Italian word, but the pottery was intended to have its own identity. Minton in particular produced monumental garden pieces which, because of the thick colours, have retained their original magnificence even when exposed to the elements.

27

with raised motifs and some gilding. Jackfield itself is on the River Severn near Coalport, but the name was used for black-glazed wares made elsewhere as well, especially in Shropshire. Jackfield ware dates from about 1740 to 1780. Cream-coloured earthenware was given semitransparent colour glazes. Brown, blue, and green combined to give a tortoiseshell colour that was popular 1740–80; the unmarked pieces are sometimes attributed to a master potter named Thomas Whieldon, after whom this mildly interesting ware is named. Opaque overglaze colours superceded Whieldon ware about 1780.

Stoneware, a German invention, is perhaps the most robust of the earlier ceramic forms. Unlike earthenware it does not need glazing to make it waterproof, but demands a high firing temperature of 1300 degrees Centigrade. By the fourteenth century salt was thrown on it in the hot kiln to form a glaze, giving an appealing orange-peel texture. The English added white Devon clay and ground flint to the clay to produce an agreeable whiteness, not unlike the white of porcelain, though lacking its fineness and translucence. Red stoneware of the highest refinement was imported from China along with cargoes of tea; it was dutifully copied and even improved upon by the inventors of Meissen porcelain. In Britain it was known as Elers ware, after two London potters in Vauxhall who specialised in it and who went bankrupt in 1700.

German stoneware was amenable to many types of glaze, not merely salt glaze. The mottled brown glaze of Cologne ware was known in England as tigerware; blue and purple glazes were introduced about 1587. The best known of early stoneware products, the Bellarmine jug, is a round or oval-bellied jug, sometimes salt-glazed, bearing the face of an obscure cardinal. It originated in Germany but was widely produced in England, especially in Staffordshire, and by John Dwight of Fulham, who was granted a patent in 1671 for a German-type stoneware). Stoneware was used for tableware in the nineteenth century, particularly in Britain and France, and Doulton and others revived it for art pottery.

Opposite: An American cream pot impressed "C. Crolius / Manufacturer / New York," and dating from 1795–1820. It is of a type widely found on the eastern seaboard. The restraint exercised in the almost fragmentary blue decoration is perhaps typical of a nation determined to make its own way. Little of this simple type of stoneware is found in Britain or Europe of the period. Stoneware was out of favour—used for mundane items such as gin flasks—and often given an "orange peel" texture to add distinction. If one did not know its history, this pot could well be taken to be art pottery of recent years.

CHAPTER TWO

THE CHINESE INFLUENCE

Every age has its obsessions. In the age of chivalry it was the search for the Holy Grail, in the eighteenth century it was the quest for the recipe for porcelain. The secret of true, hard-paste porcelain was discovered in Europe in 1709 by an alchemist at Meissen. He had failed to find gold but he had found the next best thing.

The reason for the porcelain craze is easy to see. Imports of Chinese and Japanese porcelain had shown that Europeans were not ahead of the world, as they thought they were in nearly every other sphere. Porcelain had been imported in quantity by the East India Company for many years, and not even as a primary product. Erroneously thought of as having been used as ballast for cargoes of tea and silks, porcelain—since it is heavy and waterproof—was actually used as "flooring" to make the sailing vessels "seaworthy."

Opposite: A richly enamelled Chinese porcelain bowl with a curious division between one type of decoration and another. The mania to be able to make porcelain in the Chinese style is in one way perplexing, in another way enterprising. There is no question that there was an element of pique; the Europeans regarded China (then more often known as the Manchu Empire) as a backward country of which little was known. It seemed impertinent that the Chinese could produce ware that the Western world could not.

Left: The most common piece of Chinese or Chinese-influenced ceramic is the covered blue-and-white jar with a prunus blossom design against a background of cracked ice. It was in vogue in the Kangx period (1661–1722) and exported in huge quantities to Europe during this period, when China was opening up to the West. It was revived in China in the late nineteenth century and is still being made today for the export market, without loss of quality.

Opposite: Hanau was one of the first and most productive of the German maiolica factories, established by two Dutchmen in 1661 and operating until 1806. The early wares were crude imitations of delft with similar blue-and-white designs, but standards improved, manganese and other high-temperature colours were used (with a high risk factor), and enamel colours and gold were introduced. These jugs are decorated with charming naive subjects, the one with a genre subject, faintly Dutch in feeling, and the other depicting a vaguely medieval character. The curious rendering of the clouds seems to indicate that amateur artists were given free rein. The jugs are mounted with pewter to prevent cracking at the rims. A good white could be achieved, and maiolica remained the main rival of porcelain for domestic ware. But it was easily damaged; this can be seen at the base of the jug on the left, where the body is beginning to show through.

Below: A blue-and-white tureen and ladle bearing a traditional pagoda scene, though not the celebrated willow pattern. Blue and white speedily established itself on the dining tables of the west, as the bulk of the Chinese exports in the eighteenth century were domestic pieces, and the porcelain, replacing the crude western imitations, complemented the table silver.

The Dominance of Blue-and-White

Millions of porcelain pieces were imported to Europe in the eighteenth century, most of it blue-and-white. (The ratio was nine-tenths blue-and-white to one-tenth coloured.) Even when the European manufacture of porcelain was long established, the flow of blue-and-white from the Orient continued, though the importers had become fussier, specifying exactly what they wanted. In one year in the late eighteenth century, a hundred thousand plates were imported into the United Kingdom. These imports were restricted in pattern; in one season there were only four separate designs.

The immense popularity of blue-and-white porcelain and pottery can be traced to evolving social habits. Much imported Chinese blue-and-white was tableware, and it was found that dinner and tea services visually supplemented the silver that had begun to appear in quantity on dining and tea tables. The seventeenth and eighteenth centuries had seen great social changes. The chilly formality of upper-class life had become muted (the transition is apparent in furniture design), and meals had become a pleasurable structured activity. Women played an increasing part in society and dictated etiquette, but the most significant factor was the phenomenal popularity of tea.

The Dutch brought tea to Europe in 1610. It was used in England on very rare occasions up to the 1650s, when it could cost up to £10 ($16) a pound (at least £300 ($500) in today's money). Samuel Pepys recorded his first taste of tea in 1660; in 1669 the East India Company began to import it. The craze was on. Seven hundred thousand pounds were imported in 1726; by 1766 this figure had risen to seven million. The amount doubled by 1792, and this total doubled again within ten years.

Above: A Spode teapot with a shape clearly based on silver models. Spode was founded in 1776 at Stoke-on-Trent, Staffordshire, by Joseph Spode (1733–97). He began producing cream-coloured earthenware and, from 1783, a fine type of pearlware, whiter than Wedgwood's. Spode's underglaze transfer designs are the best of their kind. In 1833, the company was acquired by T. Garrett and W. T. Copeland, who had been a partner since 1813. The new firm, Copeland and Garratt, was later renamed W. T. Copeland & Sons Ltd., and still exists as one of the best and most productive factories in the United Kingdom. Copeland late Spode dates from about 1847.

Blue-and-white porcelain was ideal for the drinking of tea, almost an essential part of the ritual. Because tea was so expensive, teapots were very small and tea was kept locked up in caddies, sometimes with twin compartments (one for green tea, one for black tea). Not only did tea drinking encourage a range of porcelain wares but also distinctive items of furniture such as the teapot. Tea was drunk from bowls; for some time cups were without handles.

The first truly hard-paste porcelain was introduced by William Cockworthy in 1766. It was made commercially in Plymouth in 1768–1770, then in Bristol, and in New Hall from about 1781. The most celebrated factories usually made only soft-paste porcelain, customarily a mixture of ground glass and white clay. Bow "porcelain" (c. 1747–76) contained bone ash (and so qualified as early bone china); it was somewhat chalky, the glaze could be marked by a knife, and the ware was prone to staining, the worst fate that could befall a hostess. Bow claimed that its products "are said to be little inferior to those brought from China," the kind of advertising that does more harm than good. Soft-paste objects are rare today because many pieces were lost in the kiln (enamel colouring required three firings), and those that did survive production have lasted less well than hard-paste.

The pursuit of blue-and-white porcelain from the golden years is keen, perhaps too keen as experts vie with each other to authenticate unmarked specimens. Sometimes they have to rely on "wasters" (broken china dumped on site), comparing it with "possibles." Some minor factories are known only by wasters excavated recently. It might be asked whether such diligence is worthwhile, and whether rare china is coveted not for its beauty but for its scarcity

There was a good deal of interaction between Europe, China, and Japan. English china was shipped to China "in the plain" (undecorated) for decorating there, while some completed Chinese plates were enriched with gilding in Britain. Some English manufacturers were even supposed to have used up ground-up Chinese porcelain in their own mix.

Certainly some of the English blue-and-white china of the classic years is of considerably inferior quality. Colours are often blurred, the hand-painting is amateurish, and transfer-printed designs can be jerky or contain unexplained gaps. Some small factories of about a hundred workers, such as Lowestoft (1756–c. 1799), attract extra attention. Their personalized pieces, including "birth tablets," are of great value because of what they are, not because of what they look like—charming and quaint

Above: Transfer-printed designs on blue and white are innumerable, and although some, such as the Italian, are well known, others are rare. Because the process was so cheap, blue-and-white transfer ware could be made to order in small quantities for families or establishments, and there was a large export market to America of transfer ware depicting American scenes. Sometimes these were designed by jobbing artists who hardly knew where America was.

Left: Tureen and dish, from about 1750, of high quality and a good deal of individuality, with an apple finial on the tureen lid and squat hoofed feet on the tureen itself.

Overleaf: A Southwark delft blue-and-white wine bottle, dated 1628, of immense charm, and illustrating graphically how age deals with maiolica. It is damage impossible to repair successfully. Southwark pottery was established in 1618 by a Dutchman who obtained a fourteen-year monopoly for making tin-glazed earthenware in 1628. His products were usually heavily modelled and based on Ming originals, the source of the birds on this wine bottle. He was less successful with his biblical scenes.

but hardly works of art. These were often done on site when the customer actually presented himself or herself at the factory. This was one of the reasons why so much china was unmarked; the retailers did not want their customers to bypass them and go directly to the factory, and they were sufficiently powerful to call the tune.

   The major British blue-and-white factories are relatively few in number—Bow (London), Bristol, Caughley (pronounced Calf-ley), Coalport, Chelsea (which produced very little blue-and-white, as did Derby), at least eight factories in Liverpool (nearly always unmarked), Longton Hall (short-lived, only about 1749–1760), Mason (a factory to be of great importance in the early nineteenth century), New Hall, Plymouth, and Worcester. In the opinion of some experts, Worcester porcelain and crypto-porcelain (1751 onward) is the most consistently fine and interest-

Below: The Tiber pattern was one of the standard designs. Italianate scenes were very popular in Britain, whether modern or classical.

Right: The all-over pattern has tended to be less popular than pictorial scenes in blue and white, in the same way that purple and white and black and white do not have the appeal of blue and white.

Below: Blue and white were considered very suitable for toilet sets, which could be basic (jug, bowl and chamber pot) or extended to include sponge dishes and soap dishes. One of the commercial advantages of blue and white was that if something was broken it was easy to replace, not necessarily with a piece of the same pattern but the same general colour. Dark blue has become more popular than light blue since the regeneration of interest in the 1960s. This sponge dish is Edwardian with added touches of red, and the key pattern on the rim of the cover adds a certain distinction, though it is low-value pottery available at hardly more than its cost when it was new.

ing. Worcester was one of the first to use transfer printing.

The great merit of blue-and-white—pottery and porcelain alike—is that it is stable. Much blue-and-white is as fresh now as when it was made. It was often painted or printed with "underglaze" blue whereby the glaze was applied after the design; X-ray photographs have revealed that the glaze blended with the decoration until they almost became one. The blue was obtained from cobalt, imported from Germany. Cobalt was the only suitable pigment because the others were inclined to be unpredictable in their ability to resist the heat required to vitrify the glaze. Eventually red was obtained from copper, and green, brown, and black from iron.

Dozens—perhaps even hundreds—of factories, many unknown, produced blue-and-white pottery, sometimes purple-and-white, sometimes black-and-white, largely for the new industrial middle classes and the upwardly mobile "improved" working classes. To maintain interest in their wares, factories issued a huge variety of commemorative jugs and plates celebrating every event likely to be known to the mass public, including George III's recovery from madness ("Britons Rejoice, cheer up and sing and drink this Health, God save the King"), his fiftieth jubilee in 1809, and the death in childbirth of his daughter Princess Charlotte. There were also scur-

Above: Jug and basin of rather better quality than most, with its gilding and frilly edges. The jug and basin set, one of the staples in the lower-middle order of the antique trade, was predominantly a Victorian invention, and millions were made for all classes of society. Before the invention of the plumbed-in wash basin there was no alternative.

Following pages: An expansive display of pottery and porcelain including examples of Mason's ironstone. Charles James Mason (1791–1856) is one of the key names in domestic pottery, producing his ironstone from 1813. His work implies great strength and reliability, which indeed it had. Mason used blue and white as well as a range of bright lively colours. The firm failed in 1848 as other firms introduced alternatives that were not markedly different.

Above: A rather fine oval dish with an unusual border impressed with circular holes. The design is classical and probably not meant to be humorous, and the pictures are surrounded by a very busy flower pattern that adds to the charm of the piece.

rilous and antimonarchist designs when George IV ascended the throne, but royal deaths were the most salesworthy.

Blue-and-white came in thousands of designs, has no class overtones, and has never gone out of fashion. A painted piece was only as good as the painter, but the transfer drawings were often splendid. The range is immense—castles, country houses, rustic scenes, the very popular Italian vistas (the "Italian" design, still made today, is one of the favourites), quasi-Chinese scenes (the most famous being the "Willow" and "Pagoda" patterns), and many other subjects. A transfer design is executed on copper, inked, transferred onto paper under pressure, and then pressed onto the article to be decorated, either under or over the glaze, whereupon the article is returned to the kiln for a final firing. Some transferred wares have been hand-tinted afterwards. "Bats" were later used, involving bats of soft glue applied to the surface instead of paper.

Wafer-thin sections of gelatine were impressed from the copper engraving, and they were sharper than the designs on paper. Introduced about 1760, bat printing was superior to other methods; it was used by Minton and Copeland in the early nineteenth century.

The original passion for blue-and-white porcelain actually lasted less than fifty years. About 1810 earthenware manufacturers captured the market with their much less expensive and often more attractive products. To many connoisseurs, the last half of the eighteenth century saw the full flowering of English porcelain.

Bone China

The continued success of blue-and-white owed much to new hybrids. Bone china, promoted by Josiah Spode II of Stoke-on-Trent, remains to this day the basic "body" of British tableware. Sèvres had used bone china in the 1750s, but in the early nineteenth century Spode brought out a new formula incorporating china clay, stone, and lead glaze. Bone china is not "true" porcelain, but is it cheaper and more durable than soft-paste—hence its appeal to the nineteenth-century millions, particularly those who wanted to upgrade themselves socially at no great cost. The

firm of Spode was acquired by W. T. Copeland in 1833, thus the double name that appears on so much nineteenth-century blue-and-white domestic ware.

Worcester also introduced their version of bone china, but an equally important innovation was Mason's Patent Ironstone China of 1813. If ever there was an impelling name this was it, implying great strength, novelty, and china (which it wasn't). It was the perfect product for the age, though the factory failed in 1848.

It is very strange that the popularity of blue-and-white in Britain and America is due to a quirk of fate—a method to keep a ship stable. In Europe, except for the early days when Chinese porcelain was copied by Meissen and the other early porcelain factories, blue-and-white enjoyed little respect or fame. One reason perhaps is that the great European factories were sponsored, subsidised, and supported by princes and grandees, to whom naive and unostentatious ceramics were anathema. British and American factories rose and fell through the stern law of supply and demand, and posterity has judged this to be a good thing.

Top: A deep-bowled Spode saucer with an attractive scene and a flowered border. Saucers are the cheapest blue-and-white a collector can buy. The only snag is that with the process of transfer printing there may be only part of a picture if it is run-of-the-mill pottery.

Above: A classic Mason jug and rectangular tray with the full Mason palette of colours well in evidence. The demise of Mason just before the Great Exhibition of 1951 might indicate that public taste was becoming increasingly debased, but many makers of domestic pottery went under as porcelain became cheaper and cheaper. The newly rich greatly preferred porcelain as it was considered more refined.

CHAPTER THREE

THE CLASSIC PERIOD

Many ceramics of the classic period—the second half of the eighteenth century—are international in character. Their appeal crossed boundaries; they were truly European. They had one other thing in common— they were intended for the rich. We can only speculate what the common people used; the best evidence comes from genre paintings of the time, but even these are not entirely reliable since the artists themselves were somewhat between classes. It is likely that the masses used time-honoured materials such as pewter long after such materials had been rejected by their social superiors.

As with furniture and other forms of antiques, ceramics demonstrated that culture followed money. Gold and platinum were often used as highlight decoration, sometimes to an extent verging on vulgarity as factory vied with factory for the

Opposite: A Meissen porcelain ewer and basin, made for the Turkish market about 1790, with naturalistic flower decorations. The long spout and handle reflect Turkish domestic styles in a marvellous manner, and with an imagination that would make the ewer acceptable anywhere. Meissen and the other German factories had long experience of exporting to Turkey, the speciality being coffee cups without handles. So that there would be no possible chance of offending the Turks, the Meissen crossed-swords mark was replaced; it was feared that the crossed swords could be mistaken in Turkey for a Christian symbol.

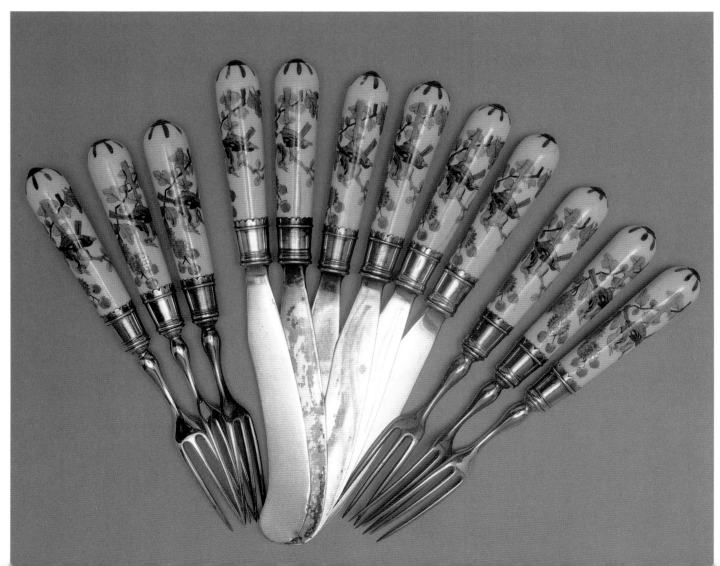

most elaborate creations. Stunning pieces were produced as new factories entered the arena and new techniques were developed and refined.

Meissen and Sèvres

With its discovery of porcelain, Meissen became the premier factory in Europe. But the Seven Years War (1756–1763) interrupted production at Meissen (Meissen is located in Saxony, and Saxony was on the losing side in this internecine war). Frederick the Great of Prussia included amongst his spoils the workmen and materials of Meissen to bolster up the factory in Berlin, and Meissen gradually yielded first place to Sèvres as the leading European manufacturer. So esteemed was the production of Sèvres that it is possible that as many Sèvres pieces were given away as prestige pieces as were sold.

Vincennes, the forerunner of Sèvres, had began production in 1738. At first it imitated Meissen style but soon specialised in flowery Rococo designs, light and airy pieces derived from the more ponderous Baroque and preceding Neoclassicism. Under the patronage of King Louis XV, Vincennes moved to Sèvres. Sèvres had a monopoly on gilding and ground colours, forbidden elsewhere by order of the king; consequently there was no competition from other French factories. New colours were constantly being introduced throughout Europe, and Sèvres was prominent in this field with their superb range of blues. Suffciently content with its magnificent soft paste, Sèvres did not initially join the rush to make hard-paste porcelain. But when good china clay was discovered at Limoges in 1768, Sèvres began their own hard-paste porcelain, turning over to hard paste completely in 1804.

Some factories had their specialties in which they reigned supreme. Beginning in

1753 Sèvres began developing biscuit, an unglazed white porcelain with a texture similar to marble and ideally suited to figures. These figures and figure groups are undisputed ceramic masterpieces. Meissen tried to copy them but without much success; it could not achieve the creamy softness of the objects made by its French counterparts.

Figures and Figure Groups

European eighteenth-century figures and figure groups represent the triumph of technique over taste, but the technique is awe-inspiring, so much so that the inevitable fakes are fairly easily spotted. Even with the aid of modern technology, few modellers today have the skill to compete with those of the past.

Porcelain figures and figure groups were extremely popular, especially in

Left: Modelled by Meissen's chief modellers, Kandler and J. F. Eberlein, this candlestick was for a service for Count Bruhl. If Sèvres had the support of the monarch, Germany had its wealthy princes. The candlestick is in Rococo style with entwined putti (cupids), and bears the coat of arms of the count. Later Meissen could be more convoluted and intricate, but this eighteenth-century piece has a restrained perfection.

Overleaf: Imari was the name given to a type of Japanese porcelain made for export at Arita and shipped from the port of Imari from the late seventeenth century onwards. Rich and full of movement, with figures and decorations tailored to European taste, Imari porcelain was not to the taste of the Japanese themselves. It was the Japanese style most often imitated in Britain, especially by Derby, Minton, Spode and Worcester throughout the eighteenth and nineteenth centuries. These imitations were not always for the best, as the natural exuberance of Imari was overlaid with Victorian trivia.

Germany. Most factories produced figures in every conceivable style and of countless subjects. Many of the characters were stereotypes. Rustic subjects such as milkmaids, if sufficiently picturesque, were coveted by the wealthy, who had probably never seen the real thing. Sugar or wax figures had been popular adornments for banquet tables, so more permanent pieces were highly sought. Figures of this type were thus modelled in the round to look good from any angle. For figures intended for the mantelpiece (a word first used in 1686) or display shelves, less attention was paid to the back, so much so that they might appear almost two-dimensional.

Because Britain lagged behind in the porcelain stakes, copies of Meissen and Sèvres were often done in soft paste and were less hard-edged. Many were accomplished with great skill; the figures of Bow, Derby, and Chelsea (Worcester produced few figures) have a quaint charm totally distinct from the virtuosity of the Europeans and, in the long run, are perhaps more endearing. Figures dominated the early work of Derby, which was initially under the influence of the European factories but gradually took on a style of its own. Chelsea figures, classed among the best, were often in the style of Sèvres.

Wedgwood

Below: Pearlware was an improved form of cream-coloured earthenware with extra flint and white clay added to the mix, and cobalt added to counteract a too warm tone. Evolved by Worcester in 1779, it was soon taken up by Spode in 1783, Leeds a little later, and Swansea in about 1800.

Some factories in Britain were not interested in producing porcelain. The most prominent of these was Wedgwood, founded by Josiah Wedgwood (1730–1795). The most distinguished English potter and the only one to exert worldwide influence, Wedgwood was a classicist who drew his inspiration from the ancient world.

Above: Wedgwood was perhaps the most adventurous of all potterys. It has survived by managing to change with the times and by demonstrating that pottery could be as important as porcelain. Through the years, its standards of good taste and quality workmanship have remained uncompromised. In its black ware (basalt) and blue ware, Wedgwood established a pottery medium that has rarely been equalled.

Left: The name of Pratt is mainly associated with potlids in collectors' minds, but F. and R. Pratt produced many charming pieces such as these cows, jug, and figures, all made between 1790 and 1810. The recumbent ram is credited to an anonymous Yorkshire pottery, but it belongs to the same period.

After apprenticeship with his brother he joined with another great potter, Thomas Whieldon, in 1754. Achieving immediate success, he enlarged his factory in 1764 and in 1769 went into partnership with a Liverpool merchant, Thomas Bentley, opening a new factory called Etruria. Not only did he realise the benefits of the Industrial Revolution by using steam power from 1782, but he also sponsored a canal system from Staffordshire to the ports of Bristol and Liverpool to facilitate his personal export drive.

Wedgwood's first great achievement was creamware, a lead-glazed ceramic with a cream-coloured body containing flint, which established itself as the best pottery body until the nineteenth century. Wedgwood was innovative and experimental; adding manganese and iron to the mix (beginning about 1769) resulted in a jet-black product that the potter named basalt, which was a great success. This led to experimentation with other ingredients, including jasper (from about 1774), originally intended for cameos but soon seen as more versatile. Jasper provided the most famous of eighteenth-century ceramics—Wedgwood blue. Pearlware was another Wedgwood development, a whiter version of creamware. Caneware and bamboo was an unglazed buff-colored earthenware modelled in narrow cylinders. Wedgwood also revived terra-cotta, an unglazed red earthenware.

Wedgwood's supreme accomplishment came in 1790 when he copied the famous Graeco-Roman cameo glass vase known as the Portland vase. He produced an edi-

Above: A Wedgwood pearlware blue and white plate made using a potting technique that involves allowing the blue to flow, giving a pleasing blurred effect. This method was almost totally confined to blue and white.

Opposite: A variety of minor pieces, including creamware, illustrating a range of attractive collectables costing very little and capable of being put to use—even practical use.

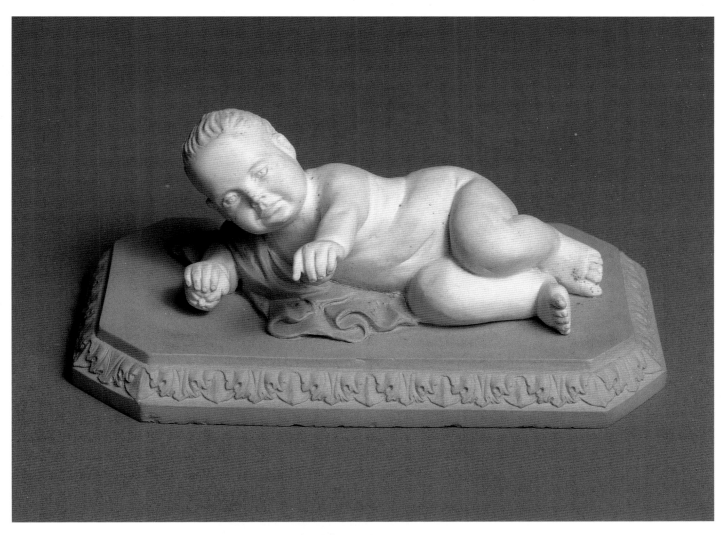

Above: A figure of a reclining child modelled by Wedgwood in three-coloured jasper, after an Italian original. It was made in about 1785 when porcelain figures were immensely popular. Wedgwood demonstrated that pottery was quite as versatile.

Left: An agreeable selection of tableware. It is sometimes interesting to see low-value pottery displayed as if it were of consequence, as it is not only clear that chain-store hollowware has some charm, but that often a good deal of effort goes into designing it. When mass-production pottery depends on large sales to be viable, manufacturers must strike a middle road between good design and low cost.

Opposite: A Wedgwood jasper lidded urn. Perfected by Wedgwood in 1775, jasperware involved adding sulphate of barium to the usual clay, making it fine grained, hard, and slightly translucent. The result was white, but the clay could be stained. Originally the stain was mixed with the clay, but after 1777, it was applied just to the surface, as this was much cheaper. In Wedgwood blue, the moulded relief figures, as here, were left white; they were not applied later, as is often believed.

tion of no more than ten, some of which did not appear until the early nineteenth century. The original vase was loaned to the British Museum, smashed by a lunatic in 1845, and painstakingly repaired and put back on show.

The Wedgwood factory has continued to make Portland vases of various sizes (six to eleven inches tall). During the prudish Victorian age, strategic drapery was introduced to cover the naughty nudity.

No other eighteenth-century European pottery even approaches the achievements of Wedgwood. Innovative and forward looking in his art, he was also ahead of his time in that he was not an elitist; he wanted to provide good pottery for all, not merely the wealthiest fraction of the population. The Europeans, obsessed with porcelain, went with the tide; technical skills were paramount. Meissen's attempts to emulate Wedgwood in porcelain were not terribly successful, but where Meissen was strong, as in its ever more naturalistic decorating, its influences on the English factories were profound.

Other European Manufacturers

Meissen had reigned supreme with its innovations in porcelain. Yet once the secret leaked out, porcelain factories were established in Vienna and Venice, as well as throughout Germany. These German factories read like a roll call of Wagnerian heroes and heroines—Frankenthal, Fürstenburg, Höchst, Ludwigsburg, and

Opposite: At first glance there might seem nothing remarkable about this shell-shaped vase, except that it seems delicately potted. It is described as vitro porcelain. In other words, it is glass! Appearances can lie. The differences between pottery, porcelain, and glass are made clear when objects are handled; the easiest way to discern the material of a piece is to flick it with a fingernail and listen to the resulting sound.

Below: An Italian teapot with an individualistic, scalloped finish of about 1725. Often overshadowed by the innovations in France and Germany, Italian pottery and porcelain has few equals. In quality, there is nothing better than Capodimonte porcelain from 1743, and although influenced by Meissen and Vienna, the potters of Capodimonte added their own Neapolitan verve. It must not be forgotten that, long before Meissen, Italian arcanists discovered the secret of porcelain manufacture, though it proved too expensive to follow through. Italian pottery and porcelain factories, particularly in Venice, were very adventurous.

Above: As porcelain became easier to make, attention moved to decoration, particularly the painting of pictures on the surface. The best artists were the equals of easel painters. Although many are forgotten, they gradually assumed the prime role formerly enjoyed by the modellers in the factories. In Britain, the painters of Worcester, such as T. Bott, are better known than the directors or even the various owners, and Hannah Barlow, an artist for Doulton, is arguably as highly rated as her contemporaries in fine art.

Nymphenburg (which made a name for itself with its ravishing figures). The luxuriant and lavish products were made regardless of expense, and many were produced for the courts of the various principalities that made up Germany.

Most countries had their own factories. Some are obscure—the Amstel, Weesp, and Oudew Loosdrecht factories of Holland are hardly names to conjure with, unlike Copenhagen, which started making soft paste in 1759 and hard paste in 1771. Russia had factories from 1758, Switzerland from 1763, and Sweden from 1777. Under the patronage of King Charles III (king of Spain from 1759 and previously king of Naples), the staff of the celebrated Capodimonte factory was transplanted wholesale to Madrid. The Naples factory, which succeeded Capidomonte, was more imaginative than most, even basing some of their porcelain on antique bronzes discovered at Herculaneum.

Potters and arcanists (those who knew the secret of making hard paste), especially from Germany, moved from factory to factory, country to country. Once figures and figure groups came to represent the acme of the potter's art, modellers were the most important individuals in the factory, and their names ring down over the years—J. C. Kändler of Ansbach, Domenica Feretti of Ludwigsburg, and E. T.

Falconet of Sèvres. Many of the men who started the factories are completely forgotten, but their employees have a place in history

It is difficult to generalise about British porcelain of the classic age. Oriental influences seem to have persisted longer in Britain than in Europe, perhaps because imports from the East were so much more numerous and were more often seen, with Japanese styles such as Imari much in evidence. British porcelain may sometimes be dismissed as provincial; or it may be that the British had more refinement and taste, as exemplified by the furniture of the period. There was no need for "power porcelain." The British did not have to prove themselves, unlike the European powers contending for major roles on the world stage. British ceramics of the eighteenth century are epitomised by the masterful output of Wedgwood—understated, functional when need be, perfectly proportioned.

The French Revolution and the Napoleonic Wars fragmented the old order, and if the aims of the revolutionaries had been realised Sèvres and the other French factories would have gone to the wall. In 1793 seven workmen were employed in smashing the stock. The potters were unpaid and often in dire penury, yet production of porcelain went on, even if the monarchs who had underwritten the enterprises were no longer there. By 1801 Napoleon had resurrected Sèvres and given it an administrator who presided for fifty years. Although it experienced a brief flowering during Napoleon's reign, Sèvres had finished its golden years, though it was to remain a major influence in all Western porcelain.

These dramatic historical events shaped the markets of the future in many and often subtle ways. The aristocratic order had been given a bloody nose, and the Napoleonic Wars reduced many nations to a state approaching penury. Even the victors, Britain and Prussia, suffered financially for a time. A hereditary ruling class, however, bounces back, even if in disguise. Luxury items remained on the agenda, as they always do in the Western world.

Left: Early eighteenth-century English delft charger, the name given to a large display plate.

CHAPTER FOUR

THE AGE OF EXUBERANCE

Nothing much changes immediately when one century clicks over to the next. The earlier years of the nineteenth century were a seamless extension of the eighteenth; only by hindsight can we see the changes waiting in the wings. In ceramics there was a shift in emphasis, especially in France. The Empire period had arrived. Perhaps an appropriate epithet for the style of the era might be "new brutalism," with the tone drawn from the person from whom the style was taken—Napoleon.

A Melange of Styles

The Neoclassical revival begun by Wedgwood was taken up but with a pedanticism and a ponderousness totally lacking in its eighteenth-century predecessor. The 1820s and 1830s witnessed an outbreak of neo-Rococo in France, Germany, and England that was a good deal more florid, even manic, than the delicate products of

Opposite: The Capodimonte porcelain factory, formed in 1743 by King Charles III of Naples, initially was influenced by Meissen and Vienna, but eventually found its own individual style, especially in figures from the Commedia dell'Arte, an Italian dramatic style based on stock characters such as Harlequin and Columbine. The Commedia dell'Arte is of considerable antiquity and influenced Shakespeare and other dramatists. The boy riding a mastiff was created by Guiseppe Gricci, the factory's chief modeller, and the humorous expression on the dog's face is characteristically Neapolitan.

the past. There was also a great interest in naturalism; shells, flowers, feathers, people, animals, and landscapes were painted with great delicacy and fidelity, some would say almost photographically. Not surprisingly, Napoleon's family was often featured by Sèvres. He had, after all, saved the factory.

These trends seem contradictory, but they set the tone for the future—mix-and-match, with features of any style bundled together, often without coherence, sometimes to show off the skills of the factory, often for display at one of the great international exhibitions that were such a feature of the second half of the nineteenth century. These display pieces—some of an unbelievable complexity and of a tastelessness unknown in the eighteenth century—were never intended to be manufactured commercially and were at one time believed to represent everyday taste. But sometimes the need for a truly grand piece for an exhibition produced a masterpiece.

Much European porcelain was revivalist, with a hunger for elaboration. The factories repeated designs from their pattern books with added extras. Novelty was all important. Sèvres pursued a new feature called "jewelling," whereby relief decoration was produced with droplets of enamel to imitate gemstones. Because the process was often used indiscriminately in low-grade products, its development was a mixed blessing. And since porcelain was no longer a luxury, there were many such poor-quality objects. Nor were new techniques possible to guard; knowledge was an international commodity.

The most skilled workers were no longer the modellers, many of whom had seen their work vandalised in the interests of commerce, but the artists. Porcelain was often used merely to show off the pictures, exemplified by the marvellous Berlin plaques, where the art is as good as in easel paintings. Subjects followed contemporary taste; reproductions of Old Master paintings, respectable but tame, were succeeded by nymphs, shepherds, and pretty girls, often nude. For sheer virtuosity there is little to equal the painting carried out at Chamberlain's (one of the three factories now in Worcester) and at nearby Coalport. Quality illustrated porcelain was widely imitated by inferior factories, and hacks were employed to do perfunctory scenes, often of incredible incompetence. There is little truly awful eighteenth-century ware; the nineteenth century was overflowing with it.

Lustre and Majolica

Although lustre painting seems to have been invented in Egypt in the seventh or eighth century, taken up in Mesopotamia and then Spain and Italy, it slipped out of fashion in the late sixteenth century. The tricky process of producing an iridescent metallic surface involved applying washes (sometimes successive) of metallic oxides (including gold and silver) onto a surface already glazed, either all over or splashed using globules of oil.

Lustre became a quintessentially early-nineteenth-century British pottery. Unlike

Above: Minton cup and saucer of traditional Japanese-influenced design using a basic blue, red, and yellow colour range. Founded in 1796, Minton first began making porcelain in 1821. Initially similar to Derby, Minton went on to become one of the most adventurous of Victorian factories, and always marked their wares even when they were making pottery in the fashionable French styles, especially Louis XVI Sèvres. Minor factories were less scrupulous.

Left: Shells have proved a powerful stimulus to designers in all fields of applied art, especially pottery, porcelain, and furniture. Their shapes are eminently suited for vases and containers, while scallops can be easily translated into dishes and trays.

Left: A Staffordshire majolica teapot in the form of a grotesque fish, dated about 1880, and accompanied by minor pieces. The workmanship is superb, and the fish scales are rendered with absolute precision. Minton also made these majolica novelty teapots. The 1870s and 1880s showed an increasing rejection of the stuffy and overblown styles that had dominated Victorian life since about 1850, and the reaction produced pottery and porcelain which is a good deal more amusing than the fun pieces of the 1930s and later.

Above: Black lustre jug and white jug with relief ornament.

much nineteenth-century ware, it precisely reflects its period. The date of its first appearance in England is uncertain. Porcelain painter and gilder John Hancock claimed that he was the inventor and that it was first used by Spode. The year of its first successful manufacture on a commercial scale dated to 1804, though lustre experimenting in England is mentioned in a book of 1772.

Lustre is especially interesting in that it was both high art and low art. Many of the jugs, trays, and other homely ware were given lengthy descriptions or mottoes, almost unique in British pottery. Lustre was practised by many factories, and perhaps the most distinctive and "period" objects were the pink-lustred Sunderland pieces, sporting engravings of the famous Wear Bridge. Sailing ships were also popular subjects. Among the most desirable lustre is Wedgwood mottled or splashed pink, probably produced until 1815, though other producers were active until at least 1850.

A distinctly English form of maiolica was introduced at the Great Exhibition of 1851 by the firm of Minton. It was now spelled majolica because it looked less alien, though it was pronounced the same.

Thomas Minton (1765–1836) supposed invented the "Willow" pattern, and his early work was cool and restrained. After French potter Léon Arnoux (1816–1902) was appointed artistic director, Minton was propelled into an innovative force. Seeking inspiration in many of the styles of the past, the factory created reworkings of Sèvres, fully marking each piece so that there would be no question that Minton

Above: Shallow bowl on the verge of art pottery with the use of flowing and overlapping coloured glazes on the base. The rather uninspired decoration on the rim is unsatisfactory. Considering the vast amount of modest pottery and porcelain that has survived, it is remarkable that errors of taste are not more common; credit must be given to that little-known species, the artistic director.

had made it (and probably Minton thought it was better than Sèvres).

Nothing was too extravagant, from a thirty-foot fountain to a complete staircase. Majolica expressed the Minton style, richly modelled and loaded with thick, luscious glazes, ideal for big household items such as umbrella stands, and jardinières for the garden. Almost indestructible, these garden pieces are frequently still in situ after nearly a hundred and fifty years.

Majolica was taken up by other British manufacturers, and in America, where E. and W. Bennett of Baltimore began production as early as 1853. Porcelain arrived late in America, and commercial production began in 1826 when William Ellis Tucker set up a factory in Philadelphia. Mass immigration brought fully trained potters to the New World, and with them came an expertise that enabled the Americans to compete on equal terms with Europe. The newly rich American middle classes were not inhibited by ideas of what they should and should not like, and took to the most audacious styles. Prinicpal American porcelain factories included Charles Cartlidge's Pottery and the Union Porcelain Company, both in New York.

V i c t o r i a n   P o r c e l a i n

To some the greatest glory of Victorian porcelain was Parian, or statuary porcelain, an echo—but a resounding one—of Sèvres biscuit ware. Parian represents

Above: The jug on the left is English, made by the Staffordshire firm of Mayer; the almost identical jug on the right is American, made by the United States Pottery Company, Bennington, Vermont. Both date from the middle of the nineteenth century, with relief figures in white against a blue background—the same general genre as Wedgwood, but without the refinement and taste. The American jug was copied from the English jug, though by this time American potteries and porcelain factories were making their own individualistic ware.

Opposite: Intended as garden ornaments or vestibule pieces, the massive Minton majolica works have a power that makes them a unique reflection of a time that was increasingly forward-looking. This peacock, as well modelled as anything in European porcelain, was designed by Comolera Paul (1818–1897). Minton employed artists of the first rank, as did most of the major factories, some of them, like Walter Crane, major easel painters. Many of them were obliged to work anonymously, but such was the demand for pottery and porcelain painters that the job security compensated for this.

Above: Hand-painted oil and vinegar bottles of some quality, with a touch of unusual modelling in the handles and nicely contrasted finials on the lids.

Opposite: Parian ware was a highly glazed white porcelain imitating marble—and imitating it very well—introduced by Copeland in 1844 and produced by all the major factories including Minton, Wedgwood and Worcester. It created a sensation at the Great Exhibtion of 1851, and this horse and rider has affinities with the horse-riding Amazon featured there.

Victorian art at its best, both in subject matter and in flawless execution. First mentioned in the magazine Art Union, Parian was originally made by Copeland and Garrett, the successors of Spode. (Copeland reverted to the Spode name in 1970, and continues to this day in partnership with Royal Worcester.) One of the earliest pieces was Narcissus designed by the fine sculptor Gibson and modelled by E. R. Stephens. Fifty copies were given as prizes by the Art Union; the cost was recorded at £3 ($5.00) each. (The Art Union was a state-approved lottery in which members drew lots for works of art in return for a modest annual subscription.)

Creating Parian was an intricate process. Liquid clay was poured into a number of moulds (sometimes as many as fifty); the pieces were then assembled using further liquid clay, and then fired at 1100 degrees Centigrade. During the process the piece contracted by a quarter of its size. It was then very lightly glazed. Parian was some-

Above: Two nineteenth-century Sèvres baluster vases with ormolu mounts. Although the flower painting is quintessentially Sèvres, the shape of the vases is somewhat Oriental, and the final effect lacks the effortless elegance associated with the factory. However, the quality of both the porcelain and the ormolu is superb; in later Sèvres, the workers in ormolu often had as much to do as the painters and the modellers. The porcelain mounts to the handles in the form of animal masks is a particularly felicitous touch, and emphasised the Chinese connection.

Opposite: The sculpting of the nude in Victorian times was a major industry in an age when exposure of the body (except where evening dresses had swooping neck lines) was considered indecent. In painting, the luscious nudes by masters such as Lord Leighton, Alma-Tadema or Poynter have been described (by critics who should know better) as soft porn. This Parian nude is of the highest quality, and was probably given a classical title to divert any possible criticism.

times used in conjunction with other materials, including porcelain, or it might be fully glazed. When the purity of Parian was fatally compromised, brass and bronze might be introduced (a Birmingham specialty).

Wedgwood and especially Minton produced Parian, as did Coalport, Worcester, and Belleek in Ireland. From the 1850s smaller manufacturers joined in, generally not marking their wares. Robinson and Leadbeater of Stoke-on-Trent was set up in 1850 solely to produce Parian, which they did well into the twentieth century, long after everyone else had all but abandoned it.

There was apparently nothing that the Victorians could not do. The supreme technical achievement was pâte-sur-pâte (paste-on-paste), developed by Sèvres in the 1860s and brought to England by Marc Louis Solon, who joined the Minton factory in 1870. The technique involves building up layer upon layer of slip on a Parian-like base, and then sculpting through the various layers. Pieces could take months to complete, and the loss in the kiln was high.

Great wealth was needed to afford such luxuries. The less well-off had to be content with mass-produced objects, commendable as they were, such as the ubiquitous blue-and-white. Many working people from all over the country visited the Great Exhibition of 1851. Enabled to afford this excursion through cheap railway fares, many such people had aspirations. They saw the pottery and porcelain on display and wanted substitutes, which the manufacturers were only too pleased to provide.

Right: A high-quality nineteenth-century candlestick of typical Rococo style and replete with cupids bearing the crossed swords of Meissen, though there must be suspicion of anything that does have such marks. Meissen was the most common mark to forge, especially in Britain where famous factories that had no need of such subterfuge were sometimes guilty. Marks can be misleading; some were applied in a hurry and bear only a passing resemblance to those in authoritative books of pottery and porcelain marks.

Above: Figure pieces were widely popular, especially amongst the poor and the lower middle class, who accepted with composure the often rudimentary modelling by journeymen and itinerant potters. Figure models were often executed by illiterate working-class artisans who often were at a loss when it came to the inscibing, resulting in amusing spelling errors. The models reflect the fact that all classes had a cultural heritage and knew even vaguely who Shakespeare's Falstaff was. It would be a brave potter who assumed the same thing today.

The display centre of the urban working-class home was the mantelpiece. Unlike the upper or middle classes, the lower classes did not have cabinets or sideboards on which to arrange their acquisitions. (Country people of moderate means might have dressers, but farm labourers lived in even meaner surroundings than their town and city counterparts and often did not even have a mantelpiece to call their own.) The need for cheap decorative objects to adorn the mantelpiece was answered by the Staffordshire potters.

Staffordshire pottery figures were popular from about 1750 to 1870, when they began to fall into decline. The figures were also made in Scotland, Wales, Liverpool, Yorkshire, and almost anywhere where a simple kiln could be installed and cheap labour was available. Staffordshire probably had a thousand potters, large and small; the work force included many unskilled women and children. The potters produced figures of contemporary people and groups depicting contemporary events. One of these groups, known as Polito's Menagerie, sold in 1987 for £7,000 ($12,250) even though it lacked two figures and a parrot.

As models, potters used the engravings in the weekly illustrated newspapers.

Below: These King Charles spaniels are "flat backs"—carved in one dimension without modelling at the back—so that they can be placed on a mantelpiece. Spaniels were exceptionally popular. They were considered an aristocratic dog and were not widely owned by the class of people who had these charming pieces on show.

Left: During the early nineteenth century when this figure was made, Napoleon was the hate figure of Britain, so it is surprising that he was perhaps the most popular subject of the Staffordshire potters. It is not much like Napoleon—the models for these figures were nothing more than weekly newspaper engravings, which themselves were executed by jobbing artists with vivid imaginations and nothing much in the way of technique.

Because the engravings themselves were sometimes poor depictions of the real subjects, the name was added at the base, either impressed, embossed, or painted. Many amusing errors resulted since a number of the caption painters were nearly illiterate.

The people or events did not have to be local; a favourite subject was the murder of the French revolutionary Jean Marat in his bath (fully clothed so as not to upset buyers). Often featured were Cobden and Peel, widely regarded as heroes of the working classes. Napoleon was perhaps the most popular of them all, though he himself was far eclipsed by the demand for pottery spaniels in pairs.

The decline in Staffordshire figures coincided with the import of cheap biscuit figures from France and Germany, lightly decorated in pastel colours, usually in early-nineteenth-century costume, and of porcelain "fairings" from Germany, compact tableaux known as "early to beds" because of their indelicate subject matter ("Shall we sleep first?"). The Japanese copied these fairings for the British market.

These cheap and cheerful novelties were called fairings for the simple reason that they were bought from a fair. Oddly enough they are of good quality, both in the manufacture and the rich colouring.

Another English specialty was the lace figure, made by dipping real lace slip before firing; the heat of the kiln then burned the lace away.

Above: A very superior model of the Italian patriot Garibaldi (1807–82), fairly late, too sophisticated for the village Staffordshire potters, and with the name embossed on the base. Garibaldi was a somewhat grizzled figure, but it was usual to smarten contemporary figures up, especially if they were heroes.

Opposite: A delightfully composed selection of Staffordshire pieces: a watch; a pot bearing an image of Prince Albert, consort to Queen Victoria; a silver shell; and a rectangular box, not to mention lavish foliage. Staffordshire pieces were made throughout the country; the most valuable are the complex pieces as here, made like a jigsaw puzzle and diligently assembled.

Items for the Masses

The concept of the souvenir was first used in its modern-day sense in 1782. Yet not until the advent of cheap railway travel that brought ready access to the seaside and other places of interest did manufacturers realise the great opportunity to make mementos for visitors to take back home with them. An inkling of this is seen in the eighteenth century with motto wares from Lowestoft bearing the words "A Trifle from Lowestoft." Cheap and cheerful, many souvenirs were made in Germany, but from about 1880 the Goss porcelain factory (established in 1858 and responsible for fine Parian ware) produced thousands of pieces of heraldic ware, marked with the coats of arms of cities, towns, and other localities. Often these came in the form of a local feature such as a castle or a statue or the font in which Shakespeare was baptised. The Goss family sold the enterprise in 1929 and it closed in 1940.

One of the most interesting group of factories in the supply of souvenirs was located in Devon, England, famous for its clay. Large-scale production was difficult because of the absence of fuel and of the industrial infrastructure that greatly assisted the factories of the north and the midlands; instead the clay was transported to areas where there was coal. In 1865 the Aller Vale pottery was set up in south

Below: Queen Victoria had two jubilees, commemorating the fiftieth and sixtieth years of her reign, in 1887 and 1897. Although her popularity had suffered when her husband Prince Albert died in 1861 and she went into prolonged mourning, she regained approval when she emerged from her trauma, and the commemorative ware reflects the respect of the nation. Although there were vulgarities, most of the pottery and porcelain, as here, were restrained.

Devon to make brownware, initially utilitarian goods such as tiles and sanitary and sewage ware, but efforts were made to channel the pottery into a new area verging on art pottery. Now known as motto ware, the brown pottery with white slip was adorned with a motto or a picture or both. Many of the mottoes had quaint Scottish overtones; others were pious proverbs. Two other potteries appeared, Watcombe (lasting 1867 to 1962) and Longpark, all providing the same kind of undemanding pottery.

Advertising was responsible for one of the most charming (and faked) ceramics. Makers of hair grease, ointments, pomades, and cosmetics realised that they could improve the visual appeal of their containers if they added transfer-applied pictorial designs. Many of these container lids were made by Pratt, a firm established in 1812 and first associated with high-quality cream-coloured earthenware painted in high-temperature colours, often over relief decorations of figures, fruit, and other motifs.

In the early nineteenth century, stoneware (sometimes salt-glazed) portrait flasks and bottles began to be made, with portraits in relief either on the side or the top half. They were ostensibly made to hold gin, the most popular spirit of the age among the poor, but it has been suggested that the poor would rather have spent

Below: The Torquay potteries of Aller Vale, Watcombe and Longpark came into existence in the late nineteenth century because of the plentiful local deposits of rich, red clay. The early work was adventurous and was more art pottery than commercial ware, though never of the quality of the London potteries; however, the three potteries later made their mark through motto ware painted in slip and enlivened with bright painting.

*Above: Three delightful pieces—an egg cup, a jug, amd a fig-
ure group—typifying the kinds of small antiques widely
available at modest cost. Egg cups in particular make a marvellous starter collection because they were produced in such
variety and quantity and take up little space.*

the money on the gin itself rather than on bottles or flasks to hold it in. Some of
the flasks bore retailers names on them, so they may primarily have been given
away, but one school of thought holds that they were created as display decorations
for pubs and gin palaces.

Dating from about 1820 to 1860, gin flasks were one of the last known items
from the Crimean War (1854–56). Like lustre ware, they are an intriguing reflection of contemporary life. The figures are almost, if not quite, as diverse as
Staffordshire figures. There are few murderers, prize-fighters, or criminals, which
were favoured subjects of the Staffordshire potters. In fact, most of the characters
are ultra-respectable—Queen Victoria and her consort, Albert; Lord Brougham,
chancellor from 1832; the celebrated American actor Thomas Rice, who became
popular in 1832; Lord Melbourne, Queen Victoria's first prime minister; and the
duke of York, who died in 1827.

The eighteenth century produced Wedgwood; the nineteenth produced Sir
Henry Doulton, a second-generation stoneware potter from Lambeth. The firm of
Doulton and Watts had been major producers of gin flasks. From the 1850s to the
1870s Sir Henry concentrated on producing glazed stoneware baths, urinals,
basins, lavatories, drain-pipes, and millions of tiles, all on a monumental scale.
Perhaps no other potter produced such an epic revolutionary effect. He pioneered
what is known as the "sanitary revolution" of the period. In an age torn apart by
periodic cholera outbreaks there is no doubt that his products saved thousands
of lives. He was also one of the first to restore the potter's self-respect in a trade
that was becoming increasingly impersonal and industrialized. In addition,
through his relationship with the Lambeth School of Art, he became one of
the founders of art pottery.

Few potters and factories were as lucky. With the decline of royal patronage—

*Previous pages: Two contrasting cups and saucers with bird
and butterfly motifs of great charm and without pretension.*

though not its disappearance—the laws of the market operated relentlessly. In former times factories could totter on for decades making relatively unwanted products, but the modern industrial world had arrived to stay. Those who failed or who had made bold but unacceptable ventures into the unknown were doomed to failure, unless underpinned by some kind of patronage. This was not uncommon; the new rich middle classes wanted to be seen on the side of culture

Thousands of pieces of Victorian display ware are still in existence, but there are far more pieces of domestic ware, mass-produced and bypassing the rage for experimentation. Much is unmarked, though some bear marks such as "Semi China" as a response to the popularity of ironstone.

Blue-and-white was produced in incredible quantity, as dinner and tea services, toilet sets comprising jug and basin and sometimes including soap trays and other accessories, chamber pots, containers of all kinds, feeding bottles, fruit comports, mugs, jugs, and indeed everything for which there was a practical purpose. Invariably these are underglazed transfer-printed pieces. They appear also in black and white, purple and white, and orange-brown and white. Although the great days of blue-and-white ended about 1840, the designs of that period continued to be used. There were even miniature dinner and tea services, sometimes made as salemen's samples but often made for children, occasionally for show.

Large institutions and companies such as railway and steamship companies, hospitals and lunatic asylums, and hotels commissioned their own ware with their names around the edge or in the centre sometimes accompanied by illustrations. Often these are minor works of art executed with great taste, and make an attractive theme collection.

Left: Stoneware had become by the nineteenth century the poor relation of the pottery family and was relegated to useful ware such as bottles and gin flasks. It was not until the later part of the nineteenth century that Doulton revived stoneware for their art pottery. These bottles are not so old as they might appear, as many brewers retained stoneware for nostalgic reasons, and because this type of pottery resists the ageing process and glazes wear well, it is often difficult to date. One has to rely on typography and stylistic anachronisms.

CHAPTER FIVE

ART POTTERY

Every age has the pottery and porcelain it deserves. Between about 1860 and 1870 there was a widespread revolt against the prevailing styles or lack of them, not only in ceramics but in furniture, upholstery, textiles, and everything that could be construed as applied art.

Opposite: Gouda is a little-known but highly rated Dutch pottery, noted for its bright colours usually applied in flat patches.

Setting the Stage

As with most rebellions this one too had a manifesto, and for better or for worse it was the architect and writer Charles Eastlake's *Hints on Household Taste in Furniture, Upholstery and other Details*, which called for the "spirit and principles of early manufacture." Published in 1868, it was widely read, even more so in America, where it appeared in 1872. The author's name became a household word, and furnishings in an "improved" taste were said to be "Eastlaked." Eastlake aimed for the "austerely picturesque . . . modern comfort and convenience." Although his own work was rather commonplace and dull and often failed to meet the criteria, he at least recognized that something had to be done about the crowded ostentation of the period.

Below: A selection of art pottery of modest pretension, red-clay based and including Torquay pottery, as in the two-handled motto beaker. The slip design on a red or brown ground, as in the tray, is a common feature of a type of art pottery veering towards the touristy, and the bird vase on the left is an example of how non-commercial pottery can go wrong.

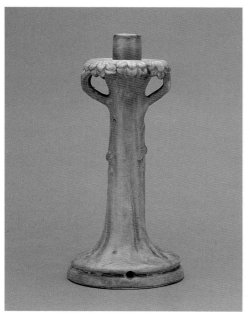

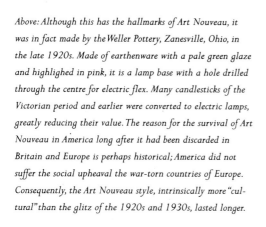

Above: Although this has the hallmarks of Art Nouveau, it was in fact made by the Weller Pottery, Zanesville, Ohio, in the late 1920s. Made of earthenware with a pale green glaze and highlighed in pink, it is a lamp base with a hole drilled through the centre for electric flex. Many candlesticks of the Victorian period and earlier were converted to electric lamps, greatly reducing their value. The reason for the survival of Art Nouveau in America long after it had been discarded in Britain and Europe is perhaps historical; America did not suffer the social upheaval the war-torn countries of Europe. Consequently, the Art Nouveau style, intrinsically more "cultural" than the glitz of the 1920s and 1930s, lasted longer.

Eastlake's predecessor, William Morris, declared that "all the minor arts were in a state of complete degradation." To help put matters right, Morris started the firm of Morris, Marshall, Faulkner & Co. in 1861; in 1875 it was renamed Morris & Co. Best known today for his wallpapers and textiles, Morris hated machinery and endeavoured to produce handmade products. Naturally these proved too expensive for his target market, the men and women with taste and discernment, and went instead to satisfy "the swinish luxury of the rich." The conflict proved too much for him and he retreated into poetic fantasy.

This was the setting for handmade art pottery, a realm in which two pieces were rarely alike, giving pleasure to both maker and owner, a seemingly impossible dream and a rejection of what passed for progress. And so it probably would have been had art pottery not been underpinned by a handful of major factory owners, principally Doulton, Wedgwood, and Minton.

Above: Aesthetic period tin-glazed oval plate with painting of languorous woman, in the style of William Crane and his school. The aesthetic period, dismissed by contemporaries as the "greenery-yellowy age" and epitomised by Oscar Wilde and Aubrey Beardsley, has no definite perimeters but was a lead-up to Art Nouveau. Its credo was art for art's sake, but with the imprisonment of Oscar Wilde and the triumph of midldle-class morality in Victorian England, it received a set-back from which it never really recovered.

London. He wrote several books, including *The Art of Decorative Design and The Development of Ornamental Art*. He became aware of the beauties of Japanese art, and travelled to Japan in 1877 to buy objects on behalf of Tiffany of New York. Japan, and, surprisingly, Peru were strong influences in the ware he designed for Linthorpe. After three years he lost interest in Linthorpe and became frenetically busy designing wallpaper, furniture, glass, textiles, and metalwork, his true vocation. In silver and silver plate he showed an inclination toward functionalism a half-century ahead of his time; he also displayed a liking for austere geometric forms as well as a pressing desire to show the works (a modernist idea still pursued with enthusiasm in architecture), as in his silver-plate teapots with exposed rivets.

Although Dresser had gone, Linthorpe went on to gain considerable public recognition, winning the Gold Medal at the Alexandra Palace Exhibition of 1883. It was a company of moderate size, employing about a hundred people at this time, but it ceased production in 1889. It influenced other art potteries, and many potters moved around what might be described as a circuit.

Bretby pottery was established in 1883 at Woodville, near Burton on Trent, by William Ault and Linthorpe's former manager, Tooth. Chunky and agreeable, Bretby pottery often featured Art Nouveau motifs in the form of glazed medallions. The Tooth–Ault combination broke up in 1887 and Ault started his own long-lasting firm. Among his designers was Christopher Dresser. Linthorpe, Bretby, and Ault therefore have very close links and resemblances, but art potteries, whatever their defects and their lack of communal spirit, are diligent in labelling their own products. To these may be added the name of Burmantoft, a Leeds pottery specializing in a heavy glazed majolica; the jardinières are more than usually striking. In 1889 two of Linthorpe's key artists and designers, Esther Ferry and Rachel Smith, joined Burmantoft, which lasted until 1904.

There are two main strands in art pottery: the heavyish no-nonsense of Linthorpe and the like, and the often airy and ethereal work carried out by men such as William de Morgan (1839–1917), long known simply as a popular novelist of the period but now remembered as perhaps the most powerful of the art potters flourishing in England. (The only pottery artist to vie with him was Walter Crane, best known for his illustrations to children's books.) Beginning in London in 1869, de Morgan decorated dishes, vases, and tiles bought in the white from the Staffordshire potteries. Learned and eclectic, he used motifs from ancient Greece, Persia, Japan, incorporating what he wanted from Art Nouveau and employing the richest of colour schemes, often in lustre. Unlike much art pottery, which depends on relief, de Morgan's work is in the flat, stylised with impeccable taste. He expanded in

Below: A teapot in the Japanese style. Many of the major potteries and porcelain factories adopted this form of design, often overpowering in its strong blues and reds.

Opposite: In the nineteenth century, it became fashionable to add the word "Crown" to the name of a porcelain factory or pottery. Crown Worcester was the first, but others followed, such as Crown Doulton, followed in due course by the minnows such as Crown Devon and Crown Dorset, which used red clay with applied designs on a creamy ground in the manner of the Torquay factories.

Below: With the exception of Delft, Arnhem was the best tin-glazed earthenware factory, originating in 1755 and closing in 1773. This plate is not from that Arnhem, but is modern.

1882, establishing a factory at Merton, and opened a factory at Fulham in 1888. He retired in 1905.

Ruskin Pottery at Smethwick, near Birmingham, was founded by W. Howson Taylor in 1898. Taylor specialized in vases and bowls in the Chinese style decorated only with simple pitted granular glazes—mottled, flambé, or monochrome. The pottery was often eggshell-like in its delicacy, the decoration applied with a tastefulness that echoed the Edwardian appreciation of fine neo-Georgian furniture.

The Pilkingtons, a coal-mining family, went into ceramics by chance. Having exhausted existing seams of coal they sought a new one, but instead of coal they found deposits of rich red clay. They decided to mine the clay for tiles, and in 1891 established Pilkington's Tile and Pottery Company, bringing in William Burton from Wedgwood to oversee the operation. Burton and his brother ran the pottery together until 1934, and in the 1970s it was amalgamated with Poole Pottery, though its golden years occurred before World War I, with an autumnal blossoming in the Art Deco period. As with Ruskin, the range of product shapes was Chinese in origin, but Pilkington employed some of the best creative talents—Walter Crane, C. F. A. Voysey (who was also a leading architect), and Lewis F. Day. The pottery painters who actually did the illustrative work were also top flight.

The pottery of Minton's Art Pottery Studio in Kensington also profited from fine artists such as W. S. Coleman, who painted in the style of Crane and is almost indistinguishable from him. Doulton continued to persevere with its stoneware. Art pottery, increasingly known as studio pottery, was clearly a success. Many commercial factories had their own art pottery division, including Howell & James, noted for its naturalist flower work; Maw & Co., for which Walter Crane created designs; Craven Dunnill & Co.; Della Robbia Pottery, named after the Italian maiolicist and famous for its bold designs; C. H. Brannam, a Linthorpe-type pottery; and Edmund Elton, a self-taught dilettante lord who used piled-on glazes on bizarre and improbable shapes and who marketed his products under the name of Sunflower Pottery, utterly quaint and British. William Moorcroft (1872–1946) set up shop in 1913, using Art Nouveau designs, which were then becoming old-fashioned, but he rediscovered slip trailing, an old English method used in the seventeenth century. If Moorcroft had a fault, his products are too much of a muchness, a phrase that could never be applied to the Martin Brothers, the eccentric fraternal band who to some represent art pottery at its outermost limit, grotesque, Gothic, weird, distinctly medieval, each piece one-of-a-kind. Grinning human faces, dysfunctional owls, strange predatory animals, malformed chessmen—almost the stuff of nightmares. Perhaps it is appropriate that the firm went out of business in the year of nightmare, 1914.

Wemyss (pronounced Weems; c. 1880–1930) made flower-adorned vases, pots, plates, and other items. The firm is most famous for its animals, often also painted

Above: A nineteenth-century atui by Meissen, used by ladies to hold needlework and other small items such as snuff spoons and pencils.

Opposite: Tile-making was one of the major Victorian industries. Great engineering projects such as the Blackwall Tunnel under the River Thames used millions of white tiles. Tiles were used on floors; on walls, often in the form of tile-pictures (still to be seen in old-fashioned unreconstructed butcher shops); on the back-splashes of wash stands; and on fireplace surrounds. The variety was and is immense, and collectors can build up a collection of hundreds without having to dig deep into their pockets. Many were made by well-known manufacturers such as Minton, but a great number are anonymous. Tiles have an advantage in that they don't have to just sit around and wait to be admired; they can be fixed into kitchen walls, as they are about the same size as modern tiles.

Above: A cake stand in the Italian maiolica colouring but not the style, which is far too prissy.

with flowers. The most desirable are the Wemyss pigs; even Franklin D. Roosevelt collected them. It may be argued that Wemyss ware is not art pottery, though some consider it so. It is agreeable if not demanding.

Few of the European potters could vie with de Morgan, Pilkington, and Ruskin, with the possible exception of Ernest Chaplet (with his marvellous array of subtle glazes), Auguste Delaherche, the Rozenburg pottery in The Hague, and the lustre ware of the Zsolnay pottery in Hungary, which owed much to the avant-garde movement known as the Austrian Secession. The Europeans too were influenced by delicate glazes, Chinese shapes, and Japanese and Art Nouveau designs, though Art Nouveau never worked as well in pottery as it did in glass. Emile Gallé did both, though his pottery hardly added to his distinction as one of the great glassmakers. Unquestionably the skills were present in Europe, but not the idiosyncrasy. The formal legacy of the past lay too heavily upon the potters.

American Art Pottery

America took to art pottery with exuberance and dash, spawning potters such as George Ohr (1857–1918), who was well ahead of his time in making large, thinly potted vessels that he crimped, folded, pinched, and crumpled until one wonders how they ever came out of the kiln in one piece. His techniques are now common-place in modern art pottery, but at the time he was unique. He may be the only potter to give up his work and become a car dealer.

The main pottery was perhaps the Rookwood Pottery of Cincinnati, established in 1880, which introduced a Japanese craftsman to work on the novel wares. One of Rookwood's most fascinating achievements was their vellum, a translucent matte glaze used for painting landscapes on plaques. The Grueby Faience Company of Boston used bold simple forms of the English Linthorpe style, with botanical designs in relief and mottled glazes.

Some art pottery was underwritten by commercial factories, as in Britain, and many creative artists primarily concerned with other fields participated, including the architect Frank Lloyd Wright, who in 1917 designed flatware for the Imperial Hotel, Tokyo, with geometric illustrations of the kind used by the painter Kandinsky. Louis Comfort Tiffany, better known for his glass, was involved in art pottery from 1904, but his products were not especially distinctive.

Art pottery is, of course, just a label. Humorous Japanese porcelain figures of the

Left: An ironstone presentation pitcher with conventional Rococo decoration, given to Mrs. Lucy Forbes. This piece is attributed to the United States Company, Bennington, Ohio, of the last half of the nineteenth century. Presentation pieces were far more common in America than in the United Kingdom. Sometimes these pitchers were called "sweetheart pitchers," a title unknown in Britain.

Left: Made by the Shawnee Pottery, Zanesville, Ohio in modified Art Deco style, this sugar bowl has decoration derived from corn motifs, apparently a standard design of this pottery. Vegetable- and fruit-shaped pottery and porcelain were always popular in Britain and Europe, even when they were less than functional, as many were designed as tureens and other tableware.

seventeenth and eighteenth centuries, the Dutch Delft tulip vases of around 1680 in the form of bizarre Turks' heads, the owl jugs of around 1700 made in Germany (so similar to Martin Brothers work), the stoneware bear jugs made in Staffordshire around 1750—all can be termed art pottery in the sense that few were made and the potters made them for pleasure, not profit. The oddest must be Castle Hedingham pottery, made by a potter named Bingham (born 1829) in a quaint ramshackle style, often mistaken as being of the sixteenth century, or even earlier. This was antiquarianism taken to its limits.

Art pottery in its classic sense faded by World War I, and when peace returned it was regarded as irrelevant and out of tune with the times, either too period or too elegiac. It seemed to lack the zip associated with the coming age of streamlining and functionalism. But potters—especially those working individually or in a small group—are traditional folk and sometimes obstinately refuse to move with the times. Art pottery is what they want to make for themselves, and if there is a market for it in the outside world so much the better.

Opposite: Fashions come and go, but one of the most consistently popular forms of pottery or china is the figure or figure group, whether it be high-fashion eighteenth-century Meissen, almost photographically accurate Sèvres, primitive Staffordshire, late-nineteenth-century porcelain from Germany, or the plethora of ornaments, often of high technical quality but little distinction, that still fill the display shelves of shops. Whatever the faults of the early Staffordshire potters, every piece was individual, and the Flight into Egypt with the Virgin Mary, Jesus, and Joseph has all the qualities and intensity of a minor masterpiece. On the yellow rectangle on the base is the single word "Flight." Had the tag been extended, there would have been problems with the foliage. Techniques lagged behind invention.

CHAPTER SIX

ART DECO AND AFTER

A rt Nouveau influenced future generations and still does. The style had not, however, proved a great spur to innovation in pottery and porcelain. The characteristic writhing shapes and plantlike forms were ill suited to potters, though not to the painters, whose work is sometimes at odds with the pottery they are actually painting.

Art Deco Arrives

After World War I a new spirit was afoot, represented by L'Exposition Internationale des Arts Décoratifs et Industriels Modernes, a great exhibition held in Paris in 1925. The name Art Deco was bestowed on the age in the 1960s. The influences on this new style came from all ages and all cultures—the Russian Ballet, Native American art, modern art movements such as Cubism and Abstraction, functional architecture promoted by the German Bauhaus, Aztec art, ancient Egypt, and the machine culture. There was little that escaped. New materials such as plastics were embraced. Its ultimate aim was to remove the old conflicts

Opposite: Art Deco and later figures in a 1930s display cabinet. The best figures were made in ivory and bronze, but because of their great expense they were manufactured in fairly small quantities. This was not the case with the porcelain figures, the most famous of which were, and are, those made by Royal Doulton, which continues to produce them.

Below: Three dancing figures. They were a favourite subject amongst modellers, for the outsplayed skirts gave the figures animation.

Opposite: Anything that has to do with golf commands high prices, and this charming pot is the equal of most golf-related artefacts that appear in auction. All golf memorabilia, except pictures, fades into insignificance when compared with the early irons, clubs, and leather-covered balls of the nineteenth century.

Below: Wall pockets of all kinds had been popular in the nineteenth century for a variety of purposes, including spill-holders, but in the twentieth century they were mainly used as vases. They were made by most of the major factories and often tastefully incorporated Art Deco motifs. The form lent itself to pleasant touches such as the "ears" by the aperture.

between art and industry and artists and artisans, and also to adapt designs to mass production.

In pottery and porcelain the new spirit was warmly embraced, not least in Britain and America. The 1920s and 1930s have been called many things: the Jazz Age, the age of the Bright Young Things, the Cocktail Age. Just as the Edwardians rejected Victorianism and all it stood for, the 1920s attempted to oust everything that was old-fashioned and outmoded. The wireless set shaped like an Aztec temple was typical of the products. Fun, bubble, and fizz were of the essence, and objects of all kinds were made to look like something else; what appeared to be a metal tennis ball opened up in segments to become an ashtray, and in pottery teapots were made in the form of racing cars or aircraft. Pottery and porcelain emphasised angularity and geometric shapes, and streamlining was seen as a very desirable feature, irrespective of whether streamlining was actually appropriate to the practical use of the object (in most cases it was obviously not).

Some of this was not new. Teapots shaped like cabbages had been made in the eighteenth century, and in the nineteenth century, in the no-man's-land between oddity and art pottery, Wedgwood had produced a quantity of quaint items, such as the 1870 three-pot inkstand in the form of an Egyptian boat, the 1867 dish and sauce tureen shaped like a shell, or the earthenware teapot naturalistically moulded

Above: For decades the flying ducks on the suburban sitting-room wall have been singled out for contempt, but, as with many innocent items (such as fairground nonsense), they have passed through their trauma and have to some degree been rehabilitated, except amongst those for whom the flying duck syndrome never went away. These are not the crumbling plaster ducks that lent the genre such a bad name, but high-quality porcelain ducks made by Poole, a modest but reliable pottery.

Righr: Four Poole vases of various shapes in the vivid colours that made such an impact during the 1930s and later.

and coloured like bamboo, with a spout in three sections—a truly Alice-in-Wonderland piece.

Hence fun was not lacking even in the dying years of Victorian excess. Wedgwood, as ever pursuing its own way and ignoring trends, has continued to produce its distinctive blue jasper with its embossed Neoclassical cameos. In 1928, suffering from a surfeit of visiting artists who were only too anxious to be employed by what must ultimately be the greatest of British factories, it produced squat vases in the Chinese style painted with formalised flowers that—except for the green, blue and silver lustre colours—would not have looked outlandish a hundred years earlier. Lustre was one of the weapons in the Wedgwood armoury; its Fairyland lustre is one of the great innovations of British pottery, delicate and otherworldly.

The fizz of Art Deco affected everybody, particularly as the 1930s succeeded the 1920s. Ordinary people saw Art Deco all around them: in that greatest of symbols, the cinema (happily many such buildings are still with us); in the "modernist" designs of department-store furniture with uncut moquette upholstery in geometrically patterned forms; in the clear-cut shapes of electrical household appliances

Above: Sardine boxes periodically turn up, and one wonders who exactly used them. Nothing has ever been written about them, and they occupy a kind of a limbo.

Opposite: Novelty ware was one of the characteristics of the post-World-War-I period, typical of which was this plate with a realistic painting of three fish.

(electric irons, vacuum cleaners, cooking ranges); in the streamlining of cars, especially American cars but also one of the unsung icons of Art Deco, the Volkswagon Beetle. Art Deco was also clearly evident in pottery and porcelain—the zigzag-shaped cups and saucers that were all but impossible to use, with ears instead of handles; the cheap plaster fairground-type vases shaped like rocket launchers, from which the colour flaked off almost immediately; and the tableware designed by the most famous name in Art Deco, Clarice Cliff.

The Three Pottery Ladies

Clarice Cliff (1900–1972) and her rivals, Charlotte Rhead and Susie Cooper, were known collectively as the three pottery ladies. The most artistic, imaginative, and high-brow of the three was Charlotte Rhead, but the work of Clarice Cliff has an exuberance and vivacity that put her well ahead of everyone else, including the well-known artists employed by the great factories. Perhaps the most extraordinary thing about Clarice Cliff is that she imbued her band of women pottery painters

Below: A jug in the shape of the face of President Herbert Hoover made by the Syracuse China Company of Syracuse, New York, between about 1928 and 1932. These jugs, made with presidents' and theatrical figures' faces on them, were a popular novelty item in the United States and are an interesting parallel to similar jugs derived from the traditional Toby jug made in the United Kingdom. An extended set of famous personages of World War I, many of them now completely unknown figures, was made in a limited edition. The Hoover jug is in yellow earthenware, glazed, and with a Hoover facsimile signature on the base.

with her own enthusiasm and energy. Her work is handpainted with geometric shapes and formalised scenes in thick, luscious colours. She designed it, often in a frenzy of activity, but credit must be paid to her workers for the end product, destined for the lucrative Woolworth's end of the market. Of course, not everybody bought Clarice Cliff. The staple market of bone china with delicate flower designs could not be dented. The "best" tea service—kept in its glazed display cabinet and used only at funerals, weddings, or anniversaries—was not amenable to change.

Cliff employed prominent artists such as Frank Brangwyn, Paul Nash, Laura Knight, Graham Sutherland, and Duncan Grant, but what endeared her to the pub-

Above: A few items from a coffee set designed by Susie Cooper, one of England's "Three Pottery ladies." She formed her own company in 1929 and it became part of the Wedgwood Group in 1966, making her wares available to a much wider public.

Above: A Clarice Cliff plate using her typical range of colours. Her work was hand painted, and she had scores of dedicated pottery painters working for her, mostly untutored women without any experience in the fine arts. Unlike her contemporary, Susie Cooper, she did not start her own company but worked for the Royal Staffordshire and Newport potteries. Her most "progressive" style, the Bizarre range, was issued in 1928.

Opposite: Clarice Cliff is the doyen of English Art Deco, a peculiarly insular style having little relevance to anything that was happening in Europe, where Art Deco was adventurous, lavish, and expensive. Clarice Cliff ware was retailed at Woolworth's for a shilling or two, and her strange shapes and bright colours were accepted immediately by the mass of the people because it was not intimidating. Cosiness was what the British public wanted, and this is what Clarice Cliff provided.

lic—and still does—were her own Bizarre, Crocus, Biarritz, and Fantasque lines. There is no one quite like her, and she embodies the best side of the between-the-wars scene.

Susie Cooper is softer than Cliff, more enamoured of pastel shades. Born in 1902, she had her own company, the Susue Cooper Pottery formed in 1929. In 1966 it became part of the Wedgwood group. Susie Cooper received the Order of the British Empire in 1079, nearly forty years after being designated a Royal Designer for Industry in 1940 for her contribution to pottery design. The award carried a certain amount of prestige, but as Britain was fighting for its life in World War II pottery was the last thing on anyones's mind. If Susie Cooper was skilled at promotion, Clarice Cliff was a boundless fount of energy and zip, Charlotte Rhead was more an art potter in the tradition of William de Morgan. Far less productive, her life is veiled in mystery; she rarely appears in any reference book and for the present she has not achieved cult status. She is what is known in espionage as a "sleeper."

International Art Deco

Many of the more innovative Art Nouveau potteries and factories found the Art Deco culture to their taste. Much was sold through specialised outlets such as the Atelier Primavera, a subsection of the Parisian store Au Printemps. Selfridges and John Lewis in London were key distributors of Susie Cooper. Severely geometric ceramics were made, with full government approval, in Leningrad (now Saint Petersburg); in the 1920s, it must be remembered, Russia had the most avant-garde art in the world. The great Russian abstract artist Malevich designed for the Russian state factories. Czech and Hungarian Art Deco was especially geometric, and somewhat serious. French Art Deco could be both witty and ponderous, sometimes too serious for its own good. Much Art Deco was not marked; if it was European and intended for Britain it might be marked "foreign," but the style was so universal that it is sometimes impossible to determine where an item comes from; indeed, something abstract and outlandish at first believed to be from some obscure European pottery may actually have been made in some obscure Staffordshire pottery.

The gaiety of Art Deco at its cheap and cheerful end is evident in Clarice Cliff's ceramic cutouts entitled The Age of Jazz; the trivial and amusing figure work often inspired by cartoon characters such as Mickey Mouse or Felix the Cat; the commercial plates celebrating some passing phase or fad; and especially the Royal Doulton figures, crafted with great flair, somewhat disdained but superbly modelled and, quite rightly, much collected. Since 1913 well over two thousand different models have been produced.

Royal Doulton figures, though not Art Deco in style, are so in feeling. True Art Deco figures are the glory of the age (as can be said of eighteenth-century Chelsea

Left: A bold corn cob with leaf jug, a motif more often used in America than in the United Kingdom.

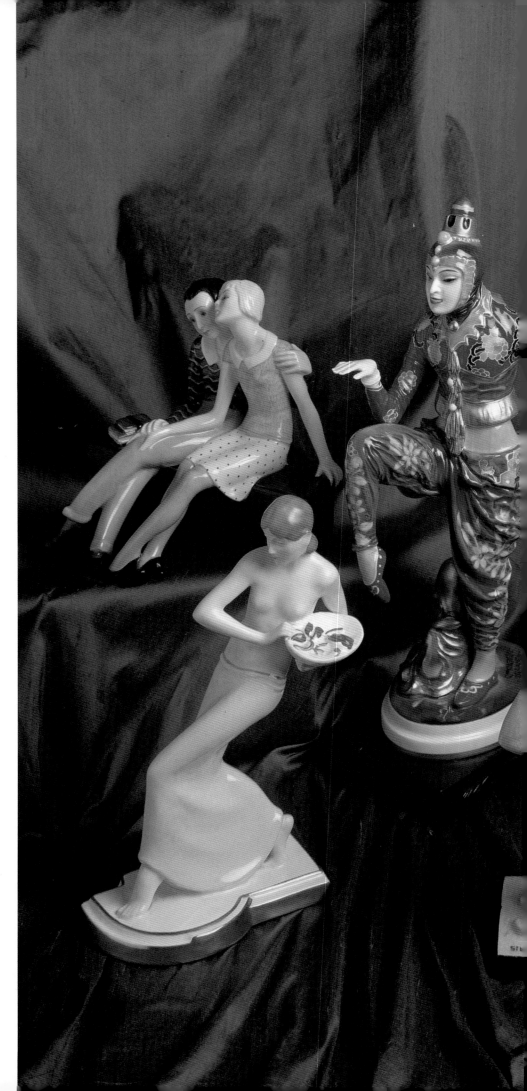

Right: A display of continental Art Deco figures. Some of the factories, such as Royal Dux, Goldscheider and Rosenthal, made a speciality of figures, but few factories pursued the genre with the tenacity of Royal Doulton, which, since 1913, has produced more than 2,000 different models. These were created by a tiny group of modellers that includes Peggy Davies, Leslie Harradine, and Mary Nicoll. To some continental factories, figure work was a passing phase only.

figures), and there are superb figures by the American Waylande de Santis Gregory, the Italian Angelo Biancini, the Frenchman Edouard-Marcel Sandoz (who designed for Limoges), and a host of factories such as Royal Dux, Zsolnay of Hungary, Goldscheider, and Rosenthal. There is only word to describe these figures and figure groups—bewitching.

Art Deco also had a quieter side. Some great potters, such as Emile Lenoble of France, ignored the zeitgeist and drew his inspiration from ancient Chinese porcelain, as did many British potters, such as Bernard Leach. Here the simple uncomplicated lines of much good Art Deco merges into studio pottery. Some of this is the polar opposite of the bright and breezy aspect of Art Deco; much of it is as understated as classic Chinese ware—dull colours, subtle glazes, the most unobtrusive of decoration, sometimes so subtle that it all but merges into the background. For better or for worse, this has continued to be a feature of art pottery to the present day. Although there is no doubting the integrity and power of master potters little known in the outside world—such as Lucie Rie, Hans Coper, Mary Rogers, Katherine Pleydell-Bouverie, William Marshall, Sam Haile, or Bernard and David Leach—there were and are so many solo potters emulating them on a shoestring (high-power electric kilns are inexpensive) that it can be a whispering rather than a shouting match as to who can be the most subdued, laid-back, and significant.

Art Deco from the United States is especially interesting. Americans were the leaders in industrial Art Deco, and this is reflected in their exuberant streamlined ware (which we can study at will in interior scenes in old black-and-white movies, a wonderful source of information). The Cowan Pottery of Ohio mass-produced ceramic objects that have all the power and finesse to be expected from high-quality

Below: A plate with bright floral designs set against a white background.

Left: A stylised rustic landscape with sunset by Poole Pottery. Although of the Art Deco period, it harks back to the late nineteenth century. This is essentially suburban ware made for the town-dweller with dreams of the rural life.

Opposite: An American money box (known in the United States as a bank) made by the McCoy Pottery Company, Roseville, Ohio, in the 1950s as a promotion aid for New York City's Emigrant Industrial Savings Bank. The eagle-shaped box is earthenware. There is a slot for coins in the eagle's back, and there is a hole in the bottom covered with removable tin and cork.

potters. Skyscrapers, sunbursts, geometric shapes, neon signs, the automobile, the cinema—all were reflected in the pottery and porcelain of the 1920s and 1930s. It may have been the age of the Great Depression, but it was also the age of jazz. The output of commercial ware in the United States was vast, little known, sometimes unmarked, but always interesting, a vast field for new collectors or for those seeking new territory to conquer.

Above: A novelty butter dish depicting a cow in a bath, a continuation of the tradition of providing a useful object in terms of something else. These are usually less efficient than articles designed with more common sense. It is doubtful whether novelty domestic ware was much used for its alleged purpose, no matter what it was.

After Art Deco

World War II marginalized pottery and porcelain. The Utility period in Britain brought the most uninteresting ceramics ever known (with the possible exception of medieval tableware), epitomised by the stoneware mugs chained to the tables in YMCAs and other canteens. The great porcelain factories of Germany were left in ruins; the factories of Bohemia—very important in the Art Deco era—came under Soviet control, thus no frills there. Crippled France could no longer rely on Sèvres for cultural sustenance.

Opposite: A tea service in the Japanese style with overlapping white panels. It features traditional motifs set against a black background broken by a gilt semi-geometric pattern.

The 1950s saw a revival of near-Deco style and pastiches have appeared ever since, but without the vitality that animated the original. Studio pottery has continued, occasionally bizarre and interesting, but basically a fringe activity of no consequence to the majority of the population. Among the mediocre productions, the long-running saga of blue-and-white and Wedgwood blue, the sensitive and consistent bone china by such firms as Spode, and the superb modern Chinese porcelain imported by the upper-end markets in great quantities stands out as something special. It is as though history is enjoying a rerun. Many types of pottery have been rediscovered; the appearance of novelty—if not the reality—is of an enduring appeal to the human race.

Previous pages: It is salutary to see how time-honoured techniques have been debased to produce seaside ware. At least this jug and plate lack the sleaze of the true candy-floss culture.

INDEX

PICTURE CREDITS

Lesley and Roy Adkins Picture Library 22

Ancient Art and Architecture Collection
9, 10, 11, 12, 13, 14, 15, 16, 17, 18, 19,
20 (left & right), 21

Christie's Images
6, 7, 8, 23, 24, 25, 33, 36–37, 38, 46, 47, 48, 49, 50–51, 57 (top), 59, 62,
63, 64, 70, 74

Esto Photographics
29, 71, 88 (top & bottom left), 91 (right), 101, 103, 112, 120

MC Picture Library
26, 27, 28, 35, 39, 40 (top & bottom), 41, 42–43, 44, 45, 52, 53,
54, 56, 57 (bottom), 58, 60, 65 (left & right), 66–67, 69, 72,
76 (left), 77, 78, 79 (left & right), 81, 82–83, 85, 86, 88–89, 90–91,
92, 93, 94, 95, 96, 97, 98,104, 106, 107, 108 (top), 108–109, 110,
111, 114, 115, 116, 117, 118–119, 121 (left & right), 122, 124–125

Ronald Pearsall
53 (bottom), 61, 87, 99, 102, 105

The Wright Family Collection
30, 31, 32, 34, 45 (bottom), 55, 68, 73,
75, 76, 80, 84, 100, 113, 123, 125